NATIONAL SYSTEM OF POLITICAL ECONOMY

VOLUME 3:
THE SYSTEMS AND THE POLITICS

FRIEDRICH LIST

COSIMO CLASSICS

NEW YORK

National System of Political Economy
Volume 3: The Systems and The Politics
Cover © 2005 by Cosimo, Inc.

National System of Political Economy,
Volume 3: The Systems and The Politics
was originally published in 1841.

For information, address:
P.O. Box 416, Old Chelsea Station
New York, NY 10011

or visit our website at:
www.cosimobooks.com

Ordering Information:
Cosimo publications are available at online bookstores. They may
also be purchased for educational, business or promotional use:
- *Bulk orders:* special discounts are available on bulk orders for reading
groups, organizations, businesses, and others. For details contact
Cosimo Special Sales at the address above or at info@cosimobooks.com.
- *Custom-label orders:* we can prepare selected books with your cover or
logo of choice. For more information, please contact Cosimo at
info@cosimobooks.com.

ISBN: 1-596-05544-8

Contents

The National Economists of Italy 5

The Industrial System (Falsely Termed by the School 'The Mercantile System') 14

The Physiocratic or Agricultural System 21

The System of Values of Exchange (Falsely Termed by the School, The 'Industrial' System) — Adam Smith 25

The System of Values of Exchange (Continued) — Jean Baptiste Say and his School 31

The Insular Supremacy and the Continental Powers — North America and France 43

The Insular Supremacy and the German Commercial Union 71

Continental Politics 96

The Commercial Policy of the German Zollverein 113

Third Book

The Systems

4

Chapter 28
The National Economists of Italy

Italy has been the forerunner of all modern nations, in the theory as well as in the practice of Political Economy. Count Pechio has given us a laboriously written sketch of that branch of Italian literature; only his book is open to the observation, that he has clung too slavishly to the popular theory, and has not duly set forth the fundamental causes of the decline of Italy's national industry — the absence of national unity, surrounded as she was by great nationalities united under hereditary monarchies; further, priestly rule and the downfall of municipal freedom in the Italian republics and cities. If he had more deeply investigated these causes, he could not have failed to apprehend the special tendency of the 'Prince' of Macchiavelli, and he would not have passed that author by with merely an incidental reference to him.(1*)

Through a remark of Pechio, that Macchiavelli in a letter to his friend Guicciardini (in 1525) had proposed a union of all the Powers of Italy against the foreigner, and that as that letter was communicated to Pope Clement VII he had thus exercised considerable influence in the formation of the 'Holy League' (in 1526), we were led to imagine that the same tendency must underlie the 'Prince.' As soon as we referred to that work, we found our anticipation confirmed at first sight. The object of the 'Prince' (written in 1513) was clearly to impress the Medici with the idea, that they were called upon to unite the whole of Italy under one sovereignty; and to indicate to them the means whereby that end might be attained. The title and form of that book, as though its general intention was to treat of the nature of absolute government, were undoubtedly selected from motives of prudence. It only alludes incidentally to the various hereditary Princes and their governments. Everywhere the author has in view only one Italian usurper. Principalities must be overthrown, dynasties destroyed, the feudal aristocracy brought under subjection, liberty in the republics rooted out. The virtues of heaven and the artifices of hell, wisdom and audacity, valour and treachery, good fortune and chance, must all be called forth, made use of, and tried by the usurper, in order to found an Italian empire. And to this end a secret is confided to him, the power of which has been thoroughly made manifest three hundred years later — a national army must be created, to whom victory must be assured by new discipline and by newly invented arms and manoeuvres.(2*)

If the general character of his arguments leaves room for doubt as to the special bias of this author, such doubt will be removed by his last chapter. There he plainly declares that foreign invasions and internal divisions are the fundamental causes of all the evils prevailing in Italy; that the House of the Medici, under whose dominion were (fortunately) Tuscany and the States of the Church, were called by Providence itself to accomplish that great work; that the present was the best time and opportunity for introducing a new régime, that now a new Moses must arise to deliver his people from the bondage of Egypt, that nothing conferred on a Prince more distinction and fame than great enterprises.(3*)

That anyone may read between the lines the tendency of that book in the other chapters also, may be best seen by the manner in which the author in his ninth chapter speaks of the States of the Church. It is merely an irony when he says, 'The priests possessed lands but did not govern them, they held lordships but did not defend them; these happiest of all territories were

6

directly protected by God's Providence, it would be presumption to utter a criticism upon them.' He clearly by this language meant it to be understood without saying so in plain words: This country presents no special impediment to a bold conqueror, especially to a Medici whose relative occupies the Papal chair.

But how can we explain the advice which Macchiavelli gives to his proposed usurper respecting the republics, considering his own republican sentiments? And must it be solely attributed to a design on his part to ingratiate himself with the Prince to whom his book is dedicated, and thus to gain private advantages, when he, the zealous republican, the great thinker and literary genius, the patriotic martyr, advised the future usurper utterly to destroy the freedom of the Italian republics? It cannot be denied that Macchiavelli, at the time when he wrote the 'Prince,' was languishing in poverty, that he regarded the future with anxiety, that he earnestly longed and hoped for employment and support from the Medici. A letter which he wrote on October 10, 1513, from his poor dwelling in the country to his friend Bettori, at Florence, places that beyond doubt.(4*)

Nevertheless, there are strong reasons for believing that he by this book did not merely design to flatter the Medici, and to gain private advantage, but to promote the realisation of a plan of usurpation; a plan which was not opposed to his republican-patriotic ideas, though according to the moral ideas of our day it must be condemned as reprehensible and wicked. His writings and his deeds in the service of the State prove that Macchiavelli was thoroughly acquainted with the history of all periods, and with the political condition of all States. But an eye which could see so far backwards, and so clearly what was around it, must also have been able to see far into the future. A spirit which even at the beginning of the sixteenth century

7

recognised the advantage of the national arming of Italy, must also have seen that the time for small republics was past, that the period for great monarchies had arrived, that nationality could, under the circumstances then existing, be won only by means of usurpation, and maintained only by despotism, that the oligarchies as they then existed in the Italian republics constituted the greatest obstacle to national unity, that consequently they must be destroyed, and that national freedom would one day grow out of national unity. Macchiavelli evidently desired to cast away the worn-out liberty of a few cities as a prey to despotism, hoping by its aid to acquire national union, and thus to insure to future generations freedom on a greater and a nobler scale.

The earliest work written specially on Political Economy in Italy, is that of Antonio Serra of Naples (in 1613), on the means of providing 'the Kingdoms' with an abundance of gold and silver.

J. B. Say and M'Culloch appear to have seen and read only the dstitle of this book: they each pass it over with the remark that it merely treats of money; and its title certainly shows that the author laboured under the error of considering the precious metals as the sole constituents of wealth. If they had read farther into it, and duly considered its contents, they might perhaps have derived from it some wholesome lessons. Antonio Serra, although he fell into the error of considering an abundance of gold and silver as the tokens of wealth, nevertheless expresses himself tolerably clearly on the causes of it.

He certainly puts mining in the first place as the direct source of the precious metals; but he treats very justly of the indirect means of acquiring them. Agriculture, manufactures, commerce, and navigation, are, according to him, the chief sources of national wealth. The fertility of the soil is a sure

8

source of prosperity; manufactures are a still more fruitful source, for several reasons, but chiefly because they constitute the foundation of an extensive commerce. The productiveness of these sources depends on the characteristic qualifications of the people (viz. whether they are industrious, active, enterprising, thrifty, and so forth), also on the nature and circumstances of the locality (whether, for instance, a city is well situated for maritime trade). But above all these causes, Serra ranks the form of government, public order, municipal liberty, political guarantees, the stability of the laws. ' No country can prosper,' says he, ' where each successive ruler enacts new laws, hence the States of the Holy Father cannot be so prosperous as those countries whose government and legislation are more stable. In contrast with the former, one may observe in Venice the effect which a system of order and legislation, which has continued for centuries, has on the public welfare.' This is the quintessence of a system of Political Economy which in the main, notwithstanding that its object appears to be only the acquisition of the precious metals, is remarkable for its sound and natural doctrine. The work of J. B. Say, although it comprises ideas and matter on Political Economy of which Antonio Serra had in his day no foreknowledge, is far inferior to Serra's on the main points, and especially as respects a due estimate of the effect of political circumstances on the wealth of nations. Had Say studied Serra instead of laying his work aside, he could hardly have maintained (in the first page of his system of Political Economy) that 'the constitution of countries cannot be taken into account in respect to Political Economy; that the people have become rich, and become poor, under every form of government; that the only important point is, that its administration should be good.'

We are far from desiring to maintain the absolute

preferableness of any one form of government compared with others. One need only cast a glance at the Southern States of America, to be convinced that democratic forms of government among people who are not ripe for them can become the cause of decided retrogression. in public prosperity. One need only look at Russia, to perceive that people who are yet in a low degree of civilisation are capable of making most remarkable progress in their national well-being under an absolute monarchy. But that in no way proves that people have become rich, i.e. have attained the highest degree of economical well-being, under all forms of government. History rather teaches us that such a degree of public well-being, namely, a flourishing state of manufactures and commerce, has been attained in those countries only whose political constitution (whether it bear the name of democratic or aristocratic republic, or limited monarchy) has secured to their inhabitants a high degree of personal liberty and of security of property whose administration has guaranteed to them a high degree of activity and power successfully to strive for the attainment of their common objects, and of steady continuity in those endeavours. For in a state of highly advanced civilisation, it is not so important that the administration should be good for a certain period, but that it should be continuously and conformably good; that the next administration should not destroy the good work of the former one; that a thirty years' administration of Colbert should not be followed by a Revocation of the Edict of Nantes, that for successive centuries one should follow one and the same system, and strive after one and the same object. Only under those political constitutions in which the national interests are represented (and not under an absolute Government, under which the State administration is necessarily always modified according to the individual will of the ruler) can such a steadiness and consistency of administration be secured, as Antonio Serra rightly observes. On the other hand, there are undoubtedly certain grades of civilisation in which the administration by absolute power may prove far more favourable to the economical and mental progress of the nation (and generally is so) than that of a limited monarchy. We refer to periods of slavery and serfdom, of barbarism and superstition, of national disunity, and of caste privileges. For, under such circumstances, the constitution tends to secure not only the interests of the nation, but also the continuance of the prevailing evils, whereas it is the interest and the nature of absolute government to destroy the latter, and it is also possible that an absolute ruler may arise of distinguished power and sagacity, who may cause the nation to make advances for centuries, and secure to its nationality existence and progress for all future time.

It is consequently only a conditional commonplace truth on the faith of which J. B. Say would exclude politics from his doctrine. In every case it is the chief desideratum that the administration should be good; but the efficiency of the administration depends on the form of government, and that form of government is clearly the best which most promotes the moral and material welfare and the future progress of any given nation. Nations have made some progress un der all forms of government. But a high degree of economical development has only been attained in those nations whose form of government has been such as to secure to them a high degree of freedom and power, of steadiness of laws and of policy, and efficient institutions.

Antonio Serra sees the nature of things as it actually exists, and not through the spectacles of previous systems, or of some one principle which he is determined to advocate and carry out. He draws a comparison between the condition of the various

States of Italy, and perceives that the greatest degree of wealth is to be found where there is extensive commerce; that extensive commerce exists where there is a well-developed manufacturing power, but that the latter is to be found where there is municipal freedom.

The opinions of beccaria are pervaded by the false doctrines of the physiocratic school. That author indeed either discovered, or derived from Aristotle, the principle of the division of labour, either before, or contemporaneously with, Adam Smith; he, however, carries it farther than Adam Smith, inasmuch as he not only applies it to the division of the work in a single manufactory, but shows that the public welfare is promoted by the division of occupation among the members of the community. At the same time he does not hesitate, with the physiocrats, to assert that manufactures are non-productive.

The views of the great philosophical jurist, Filangieri, are about the narrowest of all. Imbued with false cosmopolitanism, he considers that England, by her protective policy, has merely given a premium to contraband trade, and weakened her own commerce.

Verri, as a practical statesman, could not err so widely as that. He admits the necessity of protection to native industry against foreign competition; but did not or could not see that such a policy is conditional on the greatness and unity of the nationality.

NOTES:

1. During a journey in Germany which the author undertook while this work was in the press, he learned for the first time that Doctors Von Ranke and Gervinus have criticised Macchiavelli's Prince from the same point of view as himself.

2. Everything that Macchiavelli has written, whether before or after the publication of the Prince, indicates that he was revolving in his mind plans of this kind. How otherwise can it be explained, why he, a civilian, a man of letters, an ambassador and State official, who had never borne arms, should have occupied himself so much in studying the art of war, and that he should have been able to write a work upon it which excited the wonder of the most distinguished soldiers of his time?

3. Frederick the Great in his Anti-Macchiavel treats of the Prince as simply a scientific treatise on the rights and duties of princes generally. Here it is remarkable that he, while contradicting Macchiavelli chapter by chapter, never mentions the last or twenty-sixth chapter, which bears the heading, 'A Summons to free Italy from the Foreigners,' and instead of it inserts a chapter which is not contained in Macchiavelli's work with the heading, 'On the different kinds of Negotiations, and On the just Reasons for a Declaration of War.'

4. First published in the work, Pensieri intorno allo scopo di Nicolo Macchiavelli nel libro 'Il Principe.' Milano, 1810.

Chapter 29

The Industrial System (Falsely Termed by the School 'The Mercantile System')

At the period when great nationalities arose, owing to the union of entire peoples brought about by hereditary monarchy and by the centralisation of public power, commerce and navigation, and hence wealth and naval power, existed for the most part (as we have before shown) in republics of cities, or in leagues of such republics. The more, however, that the institutions of these great nationalities became developed, the more evident became the necessity of establishing on their own territories these main sources of power and of wealth.

Under the conviction that they could only take root and flourish under municipal liberty, the royal power favoured municipal freedom and the establishment of guilds, both which it regarded as counterpoises against the feudal aristocracy, who were continually striving for independence, and always hostile to national unity. But this expedient appeared insufficient, for one reason, because the total of the advantages which individuals enjoyed in the free cities and republics was much greater than the total of those advantages which the monarchical governments were able to offer, or chose to offer, in their own municipal cities; in the second place, because it is very difficult, indeed impossible, for a country which has always been principally engaged in agriculture, successfully to displace in free competition those countries which for centuries have acquired supremacy in manufactures, commerce, and navigation; lastly, because in the great monarchies the feudal institutions acted as hindrances to the development of their internal agriculture, and consequently to the growth of their internal manufactures. Hence, the nature of things led the great monarchies to adopt such political measures as tended to restrict the importation of foreign manufactured goods, and foreign commerce and navigation, and to favour the progress of their own manufactures, and their own commerce and navigation.

Instead of raising revenue as they had previously done by duties on the raw materials which they exported, they were henceforth principally levied on the imported manufactured goods. The benefits offered by the latter policy stimulated the merchants, seamen, and manufacturers of more highly civilised cities and countries to immigrate with their capital into the great monarchies, and stimulated the spirit of enterprise of the subjects of the latter. The growth of the national industry was followed by the growth of the national freedom. The feudal aristocracy found it necessary in their own interest to make concessions to the industrial and commercial population, as well as to those engaged in agriculture; hence resulted progress in agriculture as well as in native industry and native commerce, which had a reciprocally favourable influence on those two other factors of national wealth. We have shown how England, in consequence of this system, and favoured by the Reformation, made forward progress from century to century in the development of her productive power, freedom, and might. We have stated how in France this system was followed for some time with success, but how it came to grief there, because the institutions of feudalism, of the priesthood, and of the absolute monarchy, had not yet been reformed. We have also shown how the Polish nationality succumbed, because the elective system of monarchy did not possess influence and steadiness enough to bring into existence powerful municipal institutions, and to reform the feudal aristocracy. As a result of this policy, there was created in the place of the commercial and manufacturing city, and of the agricultural province which chiefly existed outside the political influence of that city, the agricultural-manufacturing-commercial State; a nation complete in itself, an harmonious and compact whole, in which, on the one hand, the formerly prevailing differences between monarchy, feudal aristocracy, and citizenhood gave place to one harmonious accord, and, on the other hand, the closest union and reciprocally beneficial action took place between agriculture, manufactures, and commerce. This was an immeasurably more perfect commonwealth than the previously existing one, because the manufacturing power, which in the municipal republic had been confined to a narrow range, now could extend itself over a wider sphere; because now all existing resources were placed at its disposition; because the division of labour and the confederation of the productive powers in the different branches of manufactures, as well as in agriculture, were made effectual in an infinitely greater degree; because the numerous classes of agriculturists became politically and commercially united with the manufacturers and merchants, and hence perpetual concord was maintained between them; the reciprocal action between manufacturing and commercial power was perpetuated and secured for ever; and finally, the agriculturists were made partakers of all the advantages of civilisation arising from manufactures and commerce. The agricultural-manufacturing-commercial State is like a city which spreads over a whole kingdom, or a country district raised up to be a city. In the same proportion in which material production was promoted by this union, the mental powers must necessarily have been developed, the political institutions perfected, the State revenues, the national military power, and the population, increased. Hence we see at this day, that nation which first of all perfectly developed the agricultural, manufacturing, and commercial State, standing in these respects at the head of all other nations.

The Industrial System was not defined in writing, nor was it a theory devised by authors, it was simply acted upon in practice, until the time of Stewart, who deduced it for the most part from the actual English practice, just as Antonio Serra deduced his system from a consideration of the circumstances of Venice. Stewart's treatise, however, cannot be considered a scientific work. The greater part of it is devoted to money, banking, the paper circulation — commercial crises — the balance of trade, and the doctrine of population: — discussions from which even in our day much may be learned, but which are carried on in a very illogical and unintelligible way, and in which one and the same idea is ten times repeated. The other branches of political economy are either superficially treated, or passed over altogether. Neither the productive powers, nor the elements of price, are thoroughly discussed. Everywhere the author appears to have in view only the experiences and circumstances of England. In a word, his book possesses all the merits and demerits of the practice of England, and of that of Colbert. The merits of the Industrial System as compared with later ones, are:

1. That it clearly recognises the value of native manufactures and their influence on native agriculture, commerce, and navigation, and on the civilisation and power of the nation; and expresses itself unreservedly to that effect.

2. That it indicates what is in general the right means whereby
a nation which is qualified for establishing a manufacturing power, may attain a national industry.(1*)

3. That it is based on the idea of 'the nation,' and regarding the nations as individual entities, everywhere takes into account the national interests and national conditions.

On the other hand, this system is chargeable with the following chief faults:

1. That it does not generally recognise the fundamental principle of the industrial development of the nation and the conditions under which it can be brought into operation.

2. That it consequently would mislead peoples who live in a climate unsuited for manufacturing, and small and uncivilised states and peoples, into the adoption of the protective system.

3. That it always seeks to apply protection to agriculture, and especially to the production of raw materials — to the injury of agriculture — whereas agricultural industry is sufficiently protected against foreign competition by the nature of things.

4. That it seeks to favour manufactures unjustly by imposing restrictions on the export of raw materials, to the detriment of agriculture.

5. That it does not teach the nation which has already attained manufacturing and commercial supremacy to preserve her own manufacturers and merchants from indolence, by permitting free competition in her own markets.

6. That in the exclusive pursuit of the political object, it ignores the cosmopolitical relations of all nations, the objects of the whole human race; and hence would mislead governments into a prohibitory system, where a protective one would amply suffice, or imposing duties which are practically prohibitory, when moderate protective duties would better answer the purpose. Finally.

7. That chiefly owing to his utterly ignoring the principle of cosmopolitanism, it does not recognise the future union of all nations, the establishment of perpetual peace, and of universal

freedom of trade, as the goal towards which all nations have to strive, and more and more to approach.

The subsequent schools have, however, falsely reproached this system for considering the precious metals as the sole constituents of wealth, whereas they are merely merchandise like all other articles of value; and that hence it would follow that we ought to sell as much as possible to other nations and to buy from them as little as possible.

As respects the former objection, it cannot be truly alleged of either Colbert's administration or of that of the English since George I. that they have attached an unreasonable degree of importance to the importation of the precious metals.

To raise their own native manufactures, their own navigation, their foreign trade, was the aim of their commercial policy; which indeed was chargeable with many mistakes, but which on the whole produced important results. We have observed that since the Methuen Treaty (1703) the English have annually exported great quantities of the precious metals to the East Indies, without considering these exports as prejudicial.

The Ministers of George I when they prohibited (in 1721) the importation of the cotton and silk fabrics of India did not assign as a reason for that measure that a nation ought to sell as much as possible to the foreigner, and buy as little as possible from him; that absurd idea was grafted on to the industrial system by a subsequent school; what they asserted was, that it is evident that a nation can only attain to wealth and power by the export of its own manufactured goods, and by the import from abroad of raw materials and the necessaries of life. England has followed this maxim of State policy to the present day, and by following it has become rich and mighty; this maxim is the only true one for a nation which has been long civilised, and which has already brought its own agriculture to a high degree of development.

NOTES:

1. Stewart says (book 1. chapter xxix.): 'In order to promote industry, a nation must act as well as permit, and protect. Could ever the woollen manufacture have been introduced into France from the consideration of the great advantage which England had drawn from it. if the king had not undertaken the support of it by granting many privileges to the undertakers, and by laying strict prohibitions on all foreign cloths? Is there any other way of establishing a new manufacture anywhere?'

Chapter 30

The Physiocratic or Agricultural System

Had the great enterprise of Colbert been permitted to succeed — had not the Revocation of the Edict of Nantes, the love of splendour and false ambition of Louis XIV, and the debauchery and extravagance of his successors, nipped in the bud the seeds which Colbert had sown — if consequently a wealthy manufacturing and commercial interest had arisen in France, if by good fortune the enormous properties of the French clergy had been given over to the public, if these events had resulted in the formation of a powerful lower house of Parliament, by whose influence the feudal aristocracy had been reformed — the physiocratic system would hardly have ever come to light. That system was evidently deduced from the then existing circumstances of France, and was only applicable to those circumstances.

At the period of its introduction the greater part of the landed property in France was in the hands of the clergy and the nobility It was cultivated by a peasantry languishing under a state of serfdom and personal oppression, who were sunk in superstition, ignorance, indolence, and poverty The owners of the land, who constituted its productive instruments, were devoted to frivolous pursuits, and had neither mind for, nor interest in, agriculture. The actual cultivators had neither the mental nor material means for agricultural improvements. The oppression of feudalism on agricultural production was increased by the insatiable demands made by the monarchy on the producers, which were made more intolerable by the freedom from taxation enjoyed by the clergy and nobility. Under such circumstances it was impossible that the most important branches of trade could succeed, those namely which depend on the productiveness of native agriculture, and the consumption of the great masses of the people; those only could manage to thrive which produced articles of luxury for the use of the privileged classes. The foreign trade was restricted by the inability of the material producers to consume any considerable quantity of the produce of tropical countries, and to pay for them by their own surplus produce; the inland trade was oppressed by provincial customs duties.

Under such circumstances, nothing could be more natural than that thoughtful men, in their investigations into the causes of the prevailing poverty and misery, should have arrived at the conviction, that national welfare could not be attained so long as agriculture was not freed from its fetters, so long as the owners of land and capital took no interest in agriculture, so long as the peasantry remained sunk in personal subjection, in superstition, idleness, and ignorance, so long as taxation remained undiminished and was not equally borne by all classes, so long as internal tariff restrictions existed, and foreign trade did not flourish.

But these thoughtful men (we must remember) were either physicians to the King and his Court, Court favourites, or confidants and friends of the aristocracy and the clergy they could not and would not declare open war against either absolute power or against clergy and nobility: There remained to them but one method of disseminating their views, that of concealing their plan of reform under the obscurity of a profound system, just as, in earlier as well as later times, ideas of political and religious reform have been embedded in the substance of philosophical systems. Following the philosophers of their own age and country, who, in view of the total disorganisation of the national condition of France, sought consolation in the wider field of philanthropy and cosmopolitanism (much as the father of a family, in despair at the breakup of his household, goes to seek comfort in the tavern), so the physiocrats caught at the cosmopolitan idea of universal free trade, as a panacea by which all prevailing evils might be cured. When they had got hold of this point of truth by exalting their thoughts above, they then directed them beneath, and discovered in the 'nett revenue' of the soil a basis for their preconceived ideas. Thence resulted the fundamental maxim of their system, 'the soil alone yields nett revenue' therefore agriculture is the sole source of wealth. That is a doctrine from which wonderful consequences might be inferred — first feudalism must fall, and if requisite, landowning itself; then all taxation ought to be levied on the land, as being the source of all wealth; then the exemption from taxation enjoyed by the nobility and clergy must cease; finally the manufacturers must be deemed an unproductive class, who ought to pay no taxes, but also ought to have no State-protection, hence customhouses must be abolished.

In short, people contrived by means of the most absurd arguments and contentions to prove those great truths which they had determined beforehand to prove.

Of the nation, and its special circumstances and condition in relation to other nations, no further account was to be taken, for that is clear from the 'Encyclopédie Méthodique,' which says, 'The welfare of the individual is conditional on the welfare of the entire human race.' Here, therefore, no account was taken of any nation, of any war, of any foreign commercial measures: history and experience must be either ignored or misrepresented. The great merit of this system was, that it bore the appearance of an attack made on the policy of Colbert and on the privileges of the manufacturers, for the benefit of the landowners; while in reality its blows told with most effect on the special privileges of the latter. Poor Colbert had to bear all the blame of the sufferings of the French agriculturists, while nevertheless everyone knew that France possessed a great industry for the first time since Colbert's administration; and that even the dullest intellect was aware that manufactures constitute the chief means for promoting agriculture and commerce. The Revocation of the Edict of Nantes —the wanton wars of Louis XIV — the profligate expenditure of Louis XV — were utterly ignored by these philosophers.

Quesnay in his writings has adduced, and replied to, point by point, the objections which were urged against his system. One is astonished at the mass of sound sense which he puts into the mouth of his opponents, and at the mass of mystical absurdity which he opposes to those objections by way of argument. Notwithstanding, all that absurdity was accepted as wisdom by the contemporaries of this reformer, because the tendency of his system accorded with the circumstances of France at that time, and with the philanthropic and cosmopolitan ideas prevalent in that century.

Chapter 31

The System of Values of Exchange (Falsely Termed by the School, The 'Industrial' System) — Adam Smith

Adam Smith's doctrine is, in respect to national and international conditions, merely a continuation of the physiocratic system. Like the latter, it ignores the very nature of nationalities, seeks almost entirely to exclude politics and the power of the State, presupposes the existence of a state of perpetual peace and of universal union, underrates the value of a national manufacturing power, and the means of obtaining it, and demands absolute freedom of trade.

Adam Smith fell into these fundamental errors in exactly the same way as the physiocrats had done before him, namely, by regarding absolute freedom in international trade as an axiom assent to which is demanded by common sense, and by not investigating to the bottom how far history supports this idea.

Dugald Stewart (Adam Smith's able biographer) informs us that Smith, at a date twenty-one years before his work was published in 1776 (viz. in 1755), claimed priority in conceiving the idea of universal freedom of trade, at a literary party at which he was present, in the following words:

'Man is usually made use of by statesmen and makers of projects, as the material for a sort of political handiwork. The project makers, in their operations on human affairs, disturb Nature, whereas people ought simply to leave her to herself to act freely; in order that she may accomplish her objects. In order to raise a State from the lowest depth of barbarism to the highest degree of wealth, all that is requisite is peace, moderate taxation, and good administration of justice ; everything else will follow of its own accord in the natural course of things. All governments which act in a contrary spirit to this natural course, which seek to divert capital into other channels, or to restrict the progress of the community in its spontaneous course, act contrary to nature, and, in order to maintain their position, become oppressive and tyrannical.'

Adam Smith set out from this fundamental idea, and to prove it and to illustrate it was the sole object of all his later works. He was confirmed in this idea by Quesnay, Turgot, and the other coryphaei of the physiocratic school, whose acquaintance he had made in a visit to France in the year 1765.

Smith evidently considered the idea of freedom of trade as an intellectual discovery which would constitute the foundation of his literary fame. How natural, therefore, it was that he should endeavour in his work to put aside and to refute everything that stood in the way of that idea; that he should consider himself as the professed advocate of absolute freedom of trade, and that he thought and wrote in that spirit.

How could it be expected, that with such preconceived opinions, Smith should judge of men and of things, of history and statistics, of political measures and of their authors, in any other light than as they confirmed or contradicted his fundamental principle?

In the passage above quoted from Dugald Stewart, Adam Smith's whole system is comprised as in a nutshell. The power of the State can and ought to do nothing, except to allow justice to be administered, to impose as little taxation as possible. Statesmen who attempt to found a manufacturing power, to promote navigation, to extend foreign trade, to protect it by naval power, and to found or to acquire colonies, are in his opinion project makers who only hinder the progress of the community. For him no nation exists, but merely a community, i.e. a number of individuals dwelling together. These individuals know best for themselves what branches of occupation are most to their advantage, and they can best select for themselves the means which promote their prosperity.

This entire nullification of nationality and of State power, this exaltation of individualism to the position of author of all effective power, could be made plausible only by making the main object of investigation to be not the power which effects, but the thing effected, namely, material wealth, or rather the value in exchange which the thing effected possesses. Materialism must come to the aid of individualism, in order to conceal what an enormous amount of power accrues to individuals from nationality, from national unity, and from the national confederation of the productive powers. A bare theory of values must be made to pass current as national economy, because individuals alone produce values, and the State, incapable of creating values, must limit its operations to calling into activity, protecting, and promoting the productive powers of individuals. In this combination, the quintessence of political economy may be stated as follows, viz.: Wealth consists in the possession of objects of exchangeable value; objects of exchangeable value are produced by the labour of individuals in combination with the powers of nature and with capital. By the division of labour, the productiveness of the labour is increased; capital is accumulated by savings, by production exceeding consumption. The greater the total amount of capital, so much the greater is the division of labour, and hence the capacity to produce. Private interest is the most effectual stimulus to labour and to economy. Therefore the highest wisdom of statecraft consists in placing no obstacle in the way of private industry, and in caring only for the good administration of justice. And hence also it is folly to induce the subjects of a State, by means of State legislative measures, to produce for them selves anything which they can buy cheaper from abroad. A system so consistent as this is, which sets forth the elements of wealth, which so clearly explains the process of its production, and apparently so completely exposes the errors of the previous schools, could not fail, in default of any other, to meet with acceptance. The mistake has been simply, that this system at bottom is nothing else than a system of the private economy of all the individual persons in a country, or of the individuals of the whole human race, as that economy would develop and shape itself, under a state of things in which there were no distinct nations, nationalities, or national interests — no distinctive political constitutions or degrees of civilisation — no wars or national animosities; that it is nothing more than a theory of values; a mere shopkeeper's or individual merchant's theory — not a scientific doctrine, showing how the productive powers of an entire nation can be called into existence, increased, maintained, and preserved — for the special benefit of its civilisation, welfare, might, continuance, and independence.

This system regards everything from the shopkeeper's point of view. The value of anything is wealth, according to it, so its sole object is to gain values. The establishment of powers of production, it leaves to chance, to nature, or to the providence of God (whichever you please), only the State must have nothing at all to do with it, nor must politics venture to meddle with the business of accumulating exchangeable values. It is resolved to buy wherever it can find the cheapest articles — that the home manufactories are ruined by their importation, matters not to it. If foreign nations give a bounty on the export of their manufactured goods, so much the better; it can buy them so much the cheaper. In its view no class is productive save those who actually produce things valuable in exchange. It well recognises how the division of labour promotes the success of a business in detail, but it has no perception of the effect of the division of labour as affecting a whole nation. It knows that only by individual economy can it increase its capital, and that only in proportion to the increase in its capital can it extend its individual trades; but it sets no value on the increase of the productive power, which results from the establishment of native manufactories, or on the foreign trade and national power which arise out of that increase. What may become of the entire nation in the future, is to it a matter of perfect indifference, so long as private individuals can gain wealth. It takes notice merely of the rent yielded by land, but pays no regard to the value of landed property; it does not perceive that the greatest part of the wealth of a nation consists in the value of its land and its fixed property. For the influence of foreign trade on the value and price of landed property, and for the fluctuations and calamities thence arising; it cares not a straw. In short, this system is the strictest and most consistent 'mercantile system,' and it is incomprehensible how that term could have been applied to the system of Colbert, the main tendency of which is towards an 'industrial system' -i.e. a system which has solely in view the founding of a national industry — a national commerce — without regarding the temporary gains or losses of values in exchange.

Notwithstanding, we would by no means deny the great merits of Adam Smith. He was the first who successfully applied the analytical method to political economy. By means of that method and an unusual degree of sagacity, he threw light on the most important branches of the science, which were previously almost wholly obscure. Before Adam Smith only a practice existed; his works rendered it possible to constitute a science of political economy, and he has contributed a greater amount of materials for that object than all his predecessors or successors.

But that very peculiarity of his mind by which, in analysing the various constituent parts of political economy, he rendered such important service, was the cause why he did not take a comprehensive view of the community in its entirety; that he was unable to combine individual interests in one harmonious whole; that he would not consider the nation in preference to mere individuals; that out of mere anxiety for the freedom of action of the individual producers, he lost sight of the interests of the entire nation. He who so clearly perceived the benefits of the division of labour in a single manufactory, did not perceive that the same principle is applicable with equal force to entire provinces and nations.

With this opinion, that which Dugald Stewart says of him exactly agrees. Smith could judge individual traits of character with extraordinary acuteness; but if an opinion was needed as to the entire character of a man or of a book, one could not be sufficiently astonished at the narrowness and obliquity of his views. Nay, he was incapable of forming a correct estimate of the character of those with whom he had lived for many years in the most intimate friendship. 'The portrait,' says his biographer, 'was ever full of life and expression, and had a strong resemblance to the original if one compared it with the original from a certain point of view; but it never gave a true and perfect representation according to all its dimensions and circumstances.'

Chapter 32

The System of Values of Exchange (Continued) — Jean Baptiste Say and his School

This author on the whole has merely endeavoured to systematise, to elucidate, and to popularise, the materials which Adam Smith had gathered together after an irregular fashion. In that he has perfectly succeeded, inasmuch as he possessed in a high degree the gift of systematisation and elucidation. Nothing new or original is to be found in his writings, save only that he asserted the productiveness of mental labours, which Adam Smith denied. Only, this view, which is quite correct according to the theory of the productive powers, stands opposed to the theory of exchangeable values, and hence Smith is clearly more consistent than Say. Mental labourers produce directly no exchangeable values; nay, more, they diminish by their consumption the total amount of material productions and savings, and hence the total of material wealth. Moreover, the ground on which Say from his point of view includes mental labourers among the productive class, viz. because they are paid with exchangeable values, is an utterly baseless one, inasmuch as those values have been already produced before they reach the hands of the mental labourers; their possessor alone is changed, but by that change their amount is not increased. We can only term mental labourers productive if we regard the productive powers of the nation, and not the mere possession of exchangeable values, as national wealth. Say found himself opposed to

Smith in this respect, exactly as Smith had found himself opposed to the physiocrats.

In order to include manufacturers among the productive class, Smith had been obliged to enlarge the idea of what constitutes wealth; and Say on his part had no other alternative than either to adopt the absurd view that mental labourers are not productive, as it was handed down to him by Adam Smith, or else to enlarge the idea of wealth as Adam Smith had done in opposition to the physiocrats, namely, to make it comprise productive power; and to argue, national wealth does not consist in the possession of exchangeable values, but in the possession of power to produce, just as the wealth of a fisherman does not consist in the possession of fish, but in the ability and the means of continually catching fish to satisfy his wants.

It is noteworthy, and, so far as we are aware, not generally known, that Jean Baptiste Say had a brother whose plain clear common sense led him clearly to perceive the fundamental error of the theory of values, and that J. B. Say himself expressed to his doubting brother doubts as to the soundness of his own doctrine.

Louis Say wrote from Nantes, that a technical language had become prevalent in political economy which had led to much false reasoning, and that his brother Jean himself was not free from it.(1*) According to Louis Say, the wealth of nations does not consist in material goods and their value in exchange, but in the ability continuously to produce such goods. The exchange theory of Smith and J. B. Say regards wealth from the narrow point of view of an individual merchant, and this system, which would reform the (so-called) mercantile system, is itself nothing else than a restricted mercantile system.(2*) To these doubts and objections J. B. Say replied to his brother that 'his (J. B. Say's) method (method?) (viz. the theory of exchangeable values) was certainly not the best, but that the difficulty was, to find a better.'(3*)

What! difficult to find a better? Had not brother Louis, then, found one? No, the real difficulty was that people had not the requisite acuteness to grasp and to follow out the idea which the brother had (certainly only in general terms) expressed; or rather, perhaps, because it was very distasteful to have to overturn the already established school, and to have to teach the precise opposite of the doctrine by which one had acquired celebrity. The only original thing in J. B. Say's writings is the form of his system, viz. that he defined political economy as the science which shows how material wealth is produced, distributed, and consumed. It was by this classification and by his exposition of it that J. B. Say made his success and also his school, and no wonder: for here everything lay ready to his hand; he knew how to explain so clearly and intelligibly the special process of production, and the individual powers engaged in it; he could set forth so lucidly (within the limits of his own narrow circle) the principle of the division of labour, and so clearly expound the trade of individuals. Every working potter, every huckster could understand him, and do so the more readily, the less J. B. Say told him that was new or un-known. For that in the work of the potter, hands and skill (labour) must be combined with clay (natural material) in order by means of the potter's wheel, the oven, and fuel (capital), to produce pots (valuable products or values in exchange), had been well known long before in every respectable potter's workshop, only they had not known how to describe these things in scientific language, and by means of it to generalise upon them. Also there were probably very few hucksters who did not know before J. B. Say's time, that by exchange both parties could gain values in exchange, and that if anyone

33

exported 1,000 thalers' worth of goods, and got for them 1,500 thalers' worth of other goods from abroad, he would gain 500 thalers.

It was also well known before, that work leads to wealth, and idleness to beggary; that private self-interest is the most powerful stimulus to active industry; and that he who desires to obtain young chickens, must not first eat the eggs. Certainly people had not known before that all this was political economy; but they were delighted to be initiated with so little trouble into the deepest mysteries of the science, and thus to get rid of the hateful duties which make our favourite luxuries so dear, and to get perpetual peace, universal brotherhood, and the millennium into the bargain. It is also no cause for surprise that so many learned men and State officials ranked themselves among the admirers of Smith and Say; for the principle of 'laissez faire et laissez aller' demands no sagacity from any save those who first introduced and expounded it; authors who succeeded them had nothing to do but to reiterate, embellish, and elucidate their argument; and who might not feel the wish and have the ability to be a great statesman, if all one had to do was to fold one's hands in one's bosom? It is a strange peculiarity of these systems, that one need only adopt their first propositions, and let oneself be led credulously and confidingly by the hand by the author, through a few chapters, and One is lost. We must say to M. Jean Baptiste Say at the outset that political economy is not, in our opinion, that science which teaches only how values in exchange are produced by individuals, distributed among them, and consumed by them; we say to him that a statesman will know and must know, over and above that, how the productive powers of a whole nation can be awakened, increased, and protected, and how on the other hand they are weakened, laid to sleep, or utterly destroyed; and how by means of those national productive powers the national resources can be utilised in the wisest and best manner so as to produce national existence, national independence, national prosperity, national strength, national culture, and a national future.

This system (of Say) has rushed from one extreme view that the State can and ought to regulate everything — into the opposite extreme — that the State can and ought to do nothing: that the individual is everything, and the State nothing at all. The opinion of M. Say as to the omnipotence of individuals and the impotence of the State verges on the ridiculous. Where he cannot forbear from expressing a word of praise on the efficacy of Colbert's measures for the industrial education of France, he exclaims, 'One could hardly have given private persons credit for such a high degree of wisdom.'

If we turn our attention from the system to its author, we see in him a man who, without a comprehensive knowledge of history, without deep insight into State policy or State administration, without political or philosophical views, with merely one idea adopted from others in his head, rummages through history, politics, statistics, commercial and industrial relations, in order to discover isolated proofs and facts which may serve to support his idea. If anyone will read his remarks on the Navigation Laws, the Methuen Treaty, the system of Colbert, the Eden Treaty, &c. he will find this judgment confirmed. It did not suit him to follow out connectedly the commercial and industrial history of nations. That nations have become rich and mighty under protective tariffs he admits, only in his opinion they became so in spite of that system and not in consequence of it; and he requires that we should believe that conclusion on his word alone. He maintains that the Dutch were induced to trade directly with the East Indies, because Philip II forbade

35

them to enter the harbour of Portugal; as though the protective system would justify that prohibition, as though the Dutch would not have found their way to the East Indies without it. With statistics and politics M. Say is as dissatisfied as with history: with the former because no doubt they produce the inconvenient 'facts which he says 'have so often proved contradictory of his system' — with the latter because he understood nothing at all of it. He cannot desist from his warnings against the pitfalls into which statistical facts may mislead us, or from reminding us that politics have nothing to do with political economy, which sounds about as wise as if anyone were to maintain that pewter must not be taken into account in the consideration of a pewter platter.

First a merchant, then a manufacturer, then an unsuccessful politician, Say laid hold of political economy just as a man grasps at some new undertaking when the old one cannot go on any longer. We have his own confession on record, that he stood in doubt at first whether he should advocate the (so-called) mercantile system, or the system of free trade. Hatred of the Continental system (of Napoleon) which had ruined his manufactory, and against the author of it who had turned him out of the magistracy, determined him to espouse the cause of absolute freedom of trade.

The term 'freedom' in whatever connection it is used has for fifty years past exercised a magical influence in France. Hence it happened that Say, under the Empire as well as under the Restoration, belonged to the Opposition, and that he incessantly advocated economy. Thus his writings became popular for quite other reasons than what they contained. Otherwise would it not be incomprehensible that their popularity should have continued after the fall of Napoleon, at a period when the adoption of Say's system would inevitably have ruined the

36

French manufacturers? His firm adherence to the cosmopolitical principle under such circumstances proves how little political insight the man had. How in little he knew the world, is shown by his firm belief the cosmopolitical tendencies of Canning and Huskisson. One thing only was lacking to his fame, that neither Louis XVIII nor Charles X made him minister of commerce and of finance. In that case history would have coupled his name with that of Colbert, the one as the creator of the national industry, the other as its destroyer.

Never has any author with such small materials exercised such a wide scientific terrorism as J. B. Say; the slightest doubt as to the infallibility of his doctrine was branded as obscurantism; and even men like Chaptal feared the anathemas of this politico-economical Pope. Chaptal's work on the industry of France, from the beginning to the end, is nothing else than an exposition of the effects of the French protective system; he states that expressly; he says distinctly that under the existing circumstances of the world, prosperity for France can only be hoped for under the system of protection. At the same time Chaptal endeavours by an article in praise of free trade, directly in opposition to the whole tendency of his book, to solicit pardon for his heresy from the school of Say. Say imitated the Papacy even so far as to its 'Index.' He certainly did not prohibit heretical writings individually by name, but he was stricter still; he prohibits all, the non-heretical as well as the heretical; he warns the young students of political economy not to read too many books, as they might thus too easily be misled into errors; they ought to read only a few, but those good books, which means in other words, 'You ought only to read me and Adam Smith, no others.' but that none too great sympathy should accrue to the immortal father of the school from the adoration of his disciples, his successor and interpreter on earth took good care, for, according to Say, Adam Smith's books are full of confusion, imperfection, and contradictions; and he clearly gives us to understand that one can only learn from himself 'how one ought to read Adam Smith.'

Notwithstanding, when Say was at the zenith of his fame, certain young heretics arose who attacked the basis of his system so effectually and so boldly, that he preferred privately to reply to them, and meekly to avoid any public discussion. Among these, Tanneguy du Châtel (more than once a minister of State) was the most vigorous and the most ingenious.

'Selon vous, mon cher critique,' said Say to Du Châtel in a private letter, ' il ne reste plus dans mon économie politique que des actions sans motifs, des faits sans explication, une chaîne de rapports dont les extrémités manquent et dont les anneaux les plus importants sont brisés. Je partage donc l'infortune d'Adam Smith, dont un de nos critiques a dit qu'il avait fait rétrograder l'économie politique.'(4*) In a postscript to this letter he remarks very naively, 'Dans le second article que vous annoncez, il est bien inutile de revenir sur cette polémique, par laquelle nous pouvions bien ennuyer le public.'

At the present day the school of Smith and Say has been exploded in France, and the rigid and spiritless influence of the Theory of Exchangeable Values has been succeeded by a revolution and an anarchy which neither M. Rossi nor M. Blanqui are able to exorcise. The Saint-Simonians and the Fourrierists, with remarkable talent at their head, instead of reforming the old doctrines, have cast them entirely aside, and have framed for themselves a Utopian system. Quite recently the most ingenious persons among them have been seeking to discover the connection of their doctrines with those of the previous schools, and to make their ideas compatible with existing circumstances. Important results may be expected from their labours, especially from those of the talented Michel Chevalier. The amount of truth, and of what is practically applicable in our day which their doctrines contain, consists chiefly in their expounding the principle of the confederation and the harmony of the productive powers. Their annihilation of individual freedom and independence is their weak side; with them the individual is entirely absorbed in the community, in direct contradiction to the Theory of Exchangeable Values, according to which the individual ought to be everything and the State nothing.

It may be that the spirit of the world is tending to the realisation of the state of things which these sects dream of or prognosticate; in any case, however, I believe that many centuries must elapse before that can be possible. It is given to no mortal to estimate the progress of future centuries in discoveries and in the condition of society. Even the mind of a Plato could not have foretold that after the lapse of thousands of years the instruments which do the work of society would be constructed of iron, steel, and brass, nor could that of a Cicero have foreseen that the printing press would render it possible to extend the representative system over whole kingdoms, perhaps over whole quarters of the globe, and over the entire human race. If meanwhile it is given to only a few great minds to foresee a few instances of the progress of future thousands of years, yet to every age is assigned its own special task. But the task of the age in which we live appears not to be to break up mankind into Fourrierist 'phalanstères,' in order to give each individual as nearly as possible an equal share of mental and bodily enjoyments, but to perfect the productive powers, the mental culture, the political condition, and the power of whole nationalities, and by equalising them in these respects as far as is possible, to prepare them beforehand for universal union. For even if we admit that under the existing circumstances of the world the immediate object which its apostles had in view could be attained by each 'phalanstère,' what would be its effect on the power and independence of the nation? And would not the nation which was broken up into 'phalanstères,' run the risk of being conquered by some less advanced nation which continued to live in the old way, and of thus having its premature institutions destroyed together with its entire nationality? At present the Theory of Exchangeable Values has so completely lost its influence, that it is almost exclusively occupied with inquiries into the nature of Rent, and that Ricardo in his 'Principles of Political Economy' could write, 'The chief object of political economy is to determine the laws by which the produce of the soil ought to be shared between the landowner, the farmer, and the labourer.'

While some persons are firmly convinced that this science is complete, and that nothing essential can further be added to it, those, on the other hand, who read these writings with philosophical or practical insight, maintain, that as yet there is no political economy at all, that that science has yet to be constructed; that until it is so, what goes by its name is merely an astrology, but that it is both possible and desirable out of it to produce an astronomy.

Finally, we must remark, in order not to be misunderstood, that our criticism of the writings alike of J. B. Say and of his predecessors and successors refers only to their national and international bearing; and that we recognise their value as expositions of subordinate doctrines. It is evident that an author may form very valuable views and inductions on individual branches of a science, while all the while the basis of his system may be entirely erroneous.

NOTES:

1. Louis Say, Etudes sur la Richesse des Nations, Preface, p. iv.

2. The following are the actual words of Louis Say (p. 10): 'La richesse ne consiste pas dans les choses qui satisfont nos besoins ou nos goûts, mais dans le pouvoir d'en jouir annuellement.' And further (pp. 14 to 15): 'Le faux système mercantil, fondé sur la richesse en métaux précieux, a été remplacé par un autre fondé sur la richesse en vaieurs vénales ou échangeables, qui consiste à n'évaiuer ce qui compose la richesse d'une nation que comme le fait un marchand.' And (note, p. 14): 'L'école moderne qui refute le système mercantil a elle-même créé un système qui lui-même doit être appelé le système mercantil.'

3. Etudes sur la Richesse des Nations, p. 36 (quoting J. B. Say's words): 'Que cette méthode était loin d'être bonne, mais que la difficulté était d'en trouvor une meilleure.'

4. Say, Cours complet d'Economie politique pratique, vii. p. 378.

Fourth Book

The Politics

Chapter 33

The Insular Supremacy and the Continental Powers — North America and France

In all ages there have been cities or countries which have been pre-eminent above all others in industry, commerce, and navigation; but a supremacy such as that which exists in our days, the world has never before witnessed. In all ages, nations and powers have striven to attain to the dominion of the world, but hitherto not one of them has erected its power on so broad a foundation. How vain do the efforts of those appear to us who have striven to found their universal dominion on military power, compared with the attempt of England to raise her entire territory into one immense manufacturing, commercial, and maritime city, and to become among the countries and kingdoms of the earth, that which a great city is in relation to its surrounding territory. to comprise within herself all industries, arts, and sciences; all great commerce and wealth; all navigation and naval power — a world's metropolis which supplies all nations with manufactured goods, and supplies herself in exchange from every nation with those raw materials and agricultural products of a useful or acceptable kind, which each other nation is fitted by nature to yield to her — a treasure-house of all great capital — a banking establishment for all nations, which controls the circulating medium of the whole world, and by loans and the receipt of interest on them makes all the peoples of the earth her tributaries. Let us, however, do justice to this Power and to her efforts. The world has not been hindered in its progress, but immensely aided in it, by England. She has become an example and a pattern to all nations — in internal and in foreign policy, as well as in great inventions and enterprises of every kind; in perfecting industrial processes and means of transport, as well as in the discovery and bringing into cultivation uncultivated lands, especially in the acquisition of the natural riches of tropical countries, and in the civilisation of barbarous races or of such as have retrograded into barbarism. Who can tell how far behind the world might yet remain if no England had ever existed? And if she now ceased to exist, who can estimate how far the human race might retrograde? Let us then congratulate ourselves on the immense progress of that nation, and wish her prosperity for all future time. But ought we on that account also to wish that she may erect a universal dominion on the ruins of the other nationalities? Nothing but unfathomable cosmopolitanism or shopkeepers' narrow-mindedness can give an assenting answer to that question. In our previous chapters we have pointed out the results of such denationalisation, and shown that the culture and civilisation of the human race can only be brought about by placing many nations in similar positions of civilisation, wealth, and power; that just as England herself has raised herself from a condition of barbarism to her present high position, so the same path lies open for other nations to follow: and that at this time more than one nation is qualified to strive to attain the highest degree of civilisation, wealth, and power. Let us now state summarily the maxims of State policy by means of which England has attained her present greatness. They may be briefly stated thus:

Always to favour the importation of productive power,(1*)

in preference to the importation of goods.

Carefully to cherish and to protect the development of the productive power.

To import only raw materials and agricultural products, and to export nothing but manufactured goods.

To direct any surplus of productive power to colonisation, and to the subjection of barbarous nations.

To reserve exclusively to the mother country the supply of the colonies and subject countries with manufactured goods, but in return to receive on preferential terms their raw materials and especially their colonial produce.

To devote especial care to the coast navigation; to the trade. Between the mother country and the colonies; to encourage seafisheries by means of bounties; and to take as active a part as possible in international navigation.

By these means to found a naval supremacy, and by means of it to extend foreign commerce, and continually to increase her colonial possessions.

To grant freedom in trade with the colonies and in navigation only so far as she can gain more by it than she loses.

To grant reciprocal navigation privileges only if the advantage is on the side of England, or if foreign nations can by that means be restrained from introducing restrictions on navigation in their own favour.

To grant concessions to foreign independent nations in respect import of agricultural products, only in case concessions in respect of her own manufactured products can be gained thereby.

In cases where such concessions cannot be obtained by treaty, to attain the object of them by means of contraband trade.

To make wars and to contract alliances with exclusive regard to her manufacturing, commercial, maritime, and colonial interests. To gain by these alike from friends and foes: from the latter by interrupting their commerce at sea; from the former by ruining their manufactures through subsidies which are paid in the shape of English manufactured goods.

These maxims were in former times plainly professed by all English ministers and parliamentary speakers. The ministers of George I in 1721 openly declared, on the occasion of the prohibition of the importation of the manufactures of India, that it was clear that a nation could only become wealthy and powerful if she imported raw materials and exported manufactured goods. Even in the times of Lords Chatham and North, they did not hesitate to declare in open Parliament that it ought not to be permitted that even a single horse-shoe nail should be manufactured in North America. In Adam Smith's time, a new maxim was for the first time added to those which we have above stated, namely, to conceal the true policy of England under the cosmopolitical expressions and arguments which Adam Smith had discovered, in order to induce foreign nations not to imitate that policy.

It is a very common ciever device that when anyone has attained the summit of greatness, he kicks away the ladder by which he has climbed up, in order to deprive others of the means of climbing up after him. In this lies the secret of the cosmopolitical doctrine of Adam Smith, and of the cosmopolitical tendencies of his great contemporary William Pitt, and of all his successors in the British Government administrations.

Any nation which by means of protective duties and restrictions on navigation has raised her manufacturing power and her navigation to such a degree of development that no other nation can sustain free competition with her, can do nothing wiser than to throw away these ladders of her greatness, to preach to other nations the benefits of free trade, and to declare in penitent tones that she has hitherto wandered in the paths of error, and has now for the first time succeeded in discovering the truth.

William Pitt was the first English statesman who clearly perceived in what way the cosmopolitical theory of Adam Smith could be properly made use of, and not in vain did he himself carry about a copy of the work on the Wealth of Nations. His speech in 1786, which was addressed neither to Parliament nor to the nation, but clearly to the ears of the statesmen of France, who were destitute of all experience and political insight, and solely intended to influence the latter in favour of the Eden Treaty, is an excellent specimen of Smith's style of reasoning. By nature he said France was adapted for agriculture and the production of wine, as England was thus adapted to manufacturing production. These nations ought to act towards one another just as two great merchants would do who carry on different branches of trade and who reciprocally enrich one another by the exchange of goods.(2*) Not a word here of the old maxim of England, that a nation can only attain to the highest degree of wealth and power in her foreign trade by the exchange of manufactured products against agricultural products and raw materials. This maxim was then, and has remained since, an English State secret; it was never again openly professed, but was all the more persistently followed. If, however, England since William Pitt's time had really cast away the protective system as a useless crutch, she would now occupy a much higher position than she does, and she would have got much nearer to her object, which is to monopolise the manufacturing power of the whole world. The favourable moment for attaining this object was clearly just after the restoration of the general peace. Hatred of Napoleon's Continental system had secured a reception among all nations of the Continent of the doctrines of the cosmopolitical theory. Russia, the entire North of Europe, Germany, the Spanish peninsula, and the United States of North America would have considered themselves fortunate in exchanging their agricultural produce and raw materials for English manufactured goods. France herself would perhaps have found it possible, in consideration of some decided concessions in respect of her wine and silk manufactures, to depart from her prohibitive system.

Then also the time had arrived when, as Priestley said of the English navigation laws, it would be just as wise to repeal the English protective system as it had formerly been to introduce it.

The result of such a policy would have been that all the surplus raw materials and agricultural produce from the two hemispheres would have flowed over to England, and all the world would have clothed themselves with English fabrics. All would have tended to increase the wealth and the power of England. Under such circumstances the Americans or the Russians would hardly have taken it into their heads in the course of the present century to introduce a protective system, or the Germans to establish a customs union. People would have come to the determination with difficulty to sacrifice the advantages of the present moment to the hopes of a distant future.

But Providence has taken care that trees should not grow quite up to the sky. Lord Castlereagh gave over the commercial policy of England into the hands of the landed aristocracy, and these killed the hen which had laid the golden eggs. Had they permitted the English manufactures to monopolise the markets of all nations, Great Britain would have occupied the position in respect to the world which a manufacturing town does in respect to the open country; the whole territory of the island of England would have been covered with houses and manufactories, or devoted to pleasure gardens, vegetable gardens, and orchards; to the production of milk and of meat, or of the cultivation of market produce, and generally to such cultivation as only can be carried on in the neighbourhood of great cities. The production of these things would have become much more lucrative for English agriculture than the production of corn, and consequently after a time the English landed aristocracy would have obtained much higher rents than by the exclusion of foreign grain from the home market. Only, the landed aristocracy having only their present interests in view, preferred by means of the corn laws to maintain their rents at the high rate to which they had been raised by the involuntary exclusion of foreign raw materials and grain from the English market which had been occasioned by the war; and thus they compelled the nations of the Continent to seek to promote their own welfare by another method than by the free exchange of agricultural produce for English manufactures, viz. By the method of establishing a manufacturing power of their own. The English restrictive laws thus operated quite in the same way as Napoleon's Continental system had done, only their operation was somewhat slower.

When Canning and Huskisson came into office, the landed aristocracy had already tasted too much of the forbidden fruit for it to be possible to induce them by reasons of common sense to renounce what they had enjoyed. These statesmen found themselves in the difficult position of solving an impossible problem — a position in which the English ministry still finds itself. They had at one and the same time to convince the Continental nations of the advantages of free trade, and also maintain the restrictions on the import of foreign agricultural produce for the benefit of the English landed aristocracy. Hence it was impossible that their system could be developed in such a manner that justice could be done to the hopes of the advocates of free trade on both continents. With all their liberality with philanthropical and cosmopolitical phrases which they uttered in general discussions respecting the commercial systems of England and other countries, they nevertheless did not think it inconsistent, whenever the question arose of the alteration of any particular English duties, to base their arguments on the principle of protection.

Huskisson certainly reduced the duties on several articles, but he never omitted to take care that at that lower scale of duty the home manufactories were still sufficiently protected. He thus followed pretty much the rules of the Dutch water administration. Wherever the water on the outside rises high, these wise authorities erect high dykes; wherever it rises less, they only build lower dykes. After such a fashion the reform of the English commercial policy which was announced with so much pomp reduced itself to a piece of mere politico-economical jugglery. Some persons have adduced the lowering of the English duty on silk goods as a piece of English liberality, without duly considering that England by that means only sought to discourage contraband trade in these articles to the benefit of her finances and without injury to her own silk manufactories, which object it has also by that means perfectly attained. But if a protective duty of 50 to 70 per cent (which at this day foreign silk manufacturers have to pay in England, including the extra duty(3*)) is to be accepted as a proof of liberality most nations may claim that they have rather preceded the English in that respect than followed them.

As the demonstrations of Canning and Huskisson were

specially intended to produce an effect in France and North America, it will not be uninteresting to call to mind in what way it was that they suffered shipwreck in both countries. Just as formerly in the year 1786, so also on this occasion, the English received great support from the theorists, and the liberal party in France, carried away by the grand idea of universal freedom of trade and by Say's superficial arguments, and from feelings of opposition towards a detested Government and supported by the maritime towns, the wine growers, and the silk manufacturers, the liberal party clamorously demanded, as they had done in the year 1786, extension of the trade with England as the one true method of promoting the national welfare.

For whatever faults people may lay to the charge of the Restoration, it rendered an undeniable service to France, a service which posterity will not dispute; it did not allow itself to be misled into a false step as respects commercial policy either by the stratagems of the English or by the outcry of the liberals. Mr Canning laid this business so much to heart that he himself made a journey to Paris in order to convince Monsieur Villèle of the excellence of his measures, and to induce him to imitate them. M. Villèle was, however, much too practical not to see completely through this stratagem; he is said to have replied to Mr Canning, 'If England in the far advanced position of her industry permits greater foreign competition than formerly, that policy corresponds to England's own well-understood interests. But at this time it is to the well-understood interests of France that she should secure to her manufactories which have not as yet attained perfect development, that protection which is at present indispensable to them for that object. But whenever the moment shall have arrived when French manufacturing industry can be better promoted by permitting foreign competition than by restricting it, then he (M. Villèle) would not delay to derive advantage from following the example of Mr Canning.'

Annoyed by this conclusive answer, Canning boasted in open Parliament after his return, how he had hung a millstone on the neck of the French Government by means of the Spanish intervention, from which it follows that the cosmopolitan sentiments and the European liberalism of Mr Canning were not spoken quite so much in earnest as the good liberals on the Continent might have chosen to believe. For how could Mr Canning, if the cause of liberalism on the Continent had interested him in the least, have sacrificed the liberal constitution of Spain to the French intervention owing to the mere desire to hang a millstone round the neck of the French Government? The truth is, that Mr Canning was every inch an Englishman, and he only permitted himself to entertain philanthropical or cosmopolitical sentiments, when they could prove serviceable to him in strengthening and still further extending the industry and commercial supremacy of England, or in throwing dust into the eyes of England's rivals in industry and commerce.

In fact, no great sagacity was needed on the part of M. Villèle to perceive the snare which had been laid for him by Mr Canning. In the experience of neighbouring Germany, who after the abolition of the Continental system had continually retrograded farther and farther in respect of her industry, M. Villèle possessed a striking proof of the true value of the principle of commercial freedom as it was understood in England. Also France was prospering too well under the system which she had adopted since 1815, for her to be willing to attempt, like the dog in the fable, to let go the substance and snap at the shadow. Men of the deepest insight into the condition of industry, such as Chaptal and Charles Dupin, had expressed themselves on the results of this system in the most unequivocal manner.

Chaptal's work on French industry is nothing less than a defence of the French commercial policy, and an exposition of its results as a whole and in every particular. The tendency of this work is expressed in the following quotation from it. 'Instead of losing ourselves in the labyrinth of metaphysical abstractions, we maintain above all that which exists, and seek above all to make it perfect. Good customs legislation is the bulwark of manufacturing industry. It increases or lessens import duties according to circumstances; it compensates the disadvantages of higher wages of labour and of higher prices of fuel; it protects arts and industries in their cradle until they at length become strong enough to bear foreign competition; it creates the industrial independence of France and enriches the nation through labour, which, as I have already often remarked, is the chief source of wealth.'(4*)

Charles Dupin had, in his work 'On the Productive Powers of France, and on the Progress of French Industry from 1814 to 1847,' thrown such a clear light on the results of the commercial policy which France had followed since the Restoration, that it was impossible that a French minister could think of sacrificing this work of half a century, which had cost such sacrifices, which was so rich in fruits, and so full of promise for the future, merely for the attractions of a Methuen Treaty.

The American tariff for the year 1828 was a natural and necessary result of the English commercial system, which shut out from the English frontiers the North American timber, grain, meal, and other agricultural products, and only permitted raw cotton to be received by England in exchange for her manufactured goods. On this system the trade with England only tended to promote the agricultural labour of the American slaves, while on the other hand, the freest, most enlightened, and most powerful States of the Union found themselves entirely arrested in their economical progress, and thus reduced to dispose of their annual surplus of population and capital by emigration to the waste lands of the West. Mr Huskisson understood this position of affairs very well. It was notorious that the English ambassador in Washington had more than once correctly informed him of the inevitable consequence of the English policy. If Mr Huskisson had really been the man that people in other countries supposed him to be, he would have made use of the publication of the American tariff as a valuable opportunity for making the English aristocracy comprehend the folly of their corn laws, and the necessity of abolishing them. But what did Mr Huskisson do? He fell into a passion with the Americans (or at least affected to do so), and in his excitement he made allegations — the incorrectness of which was well known to every American planter — and permitted himself to use threats which made him ridiculous. Mr Huskisson said the exports of England to the United States amounted to only about the sixth part of all the exports of England, while the exports of the United States to England constituted more than half of all their exports. From this he sought to prove that the Americans were more in the power of the English than the latter were in that of the former; and that the English had much less reason to fear interruptions of trade through war, cessation of intercourse, and so forth, than the Americans had. If one looks merely at the totals of the value of the imports and exports, Huskisson's argument appears sufficiently plausible; but if one considers the nature of the reciprocal imports and exports, it will then appear incomprehensible how Mr Huskisson could make use of an argument which proves the exact opposite of that which he desired to prove. All or by far the greater part of the exports of the United States to England consisted of raw materials, whose value is increased tenfold by the English, and which they cannot dispense with, and also could not at once obtain from other countries, at any rate not in sufficient quantity, while on the other hand all the imports of the North Americans from England consisted of articles which they could either manufacture for themselves or procure just as easily from other nations. If we now consider what would be the operation of an interruption of commerce between the two nations according to the theory of values, it will appear as if it must operate to the disadvantage of the Americans; whereas if we judge of it according to the theory of the productive powers, it must occasion incalculable injury to the English. For by it two-thirds of all the English cotton manufactories would come to a standstill and fall into ruin. England would lose as by magic a productive source of wealth, the annual value of which far exceeds the value of her entire exports, and the results of such a loss on the peace, wealth, credit, commerce, and power of England would be incalculable. What, however, would be the consequences of such a state of things for the North Americans? Compelled to manufacture for themselves those goods which they had hitherto obtained from England, they would in the course of a few years gain what the English had lost. No doubt such a measure must occasion a conflict for life and death, as formerly the navigation laws did between England and Holland. But probably it would also end in the same way as formerly did the conflict in the English Channel. It is unnecessary here to follow out the consequences of a rivalry which, as it appears to us, must sooner or later, from the very nature of things, come to a rupture. What we have said suffices to show clearly the futility and danger of Huskisson's argument, and to demonstrate how unwisely England acted in compelling the

North Americans (by means of her corn laws) to manufacture for themselves, and how wise it would have been of Mr Huskisson had he, instead of trifling with the question by such futile and hazardous arguments, laboured to remove out of the way the causes which led to the adoption of the American tariff of 1828.

In order to prove to the North Americans how advantageous to them the trade of England was, Mr Huskisson pointed out the extraordinary increase in the English importations of cotton, but the Americans also knew how to estimate this argument at its true value. For the production of cotton in America had for more than ten years previously so greatly exceeded the consumption of, and the demand for, this article from year to year, that its prices had fallen in almost the same ratio in which the export had increased; as may be seen from the fact that in the year 1816 the Americans had obtained for 80,000,000 pounds of cotton 24,000,000 dollars, while in the year 1826 for 204,000,000 pounds of cotton they only obtained 25,000,000 dollars.

Finally, Mr Huskisson threatened the North Americans with the organisation of a wholesale contraband trade by way of Canada. It is true that under existing circumstances an American protective system can be endangered by nothing so seriously as by the means indicated by Mr Huskisson. But what follows from that? Is it that the Americans are to lay their system at the feet of the English Parliament, and await in humility whatever the latter may be pleased to determine from year to year respecting their national industry? How absurd! The only consequence would be that the Americans would annex Canada and include it in their Union, or else assist it to attain independence as soon as ever the Canadian smuggling trade became unendurable. Must we not, however, deem the degree of folly absolutely excessive if a nation which has already attained industrial and commercial supremacy, first of all compels an agricultural nation connected with her by the closest ties of race, of language, and of interest, to become herself a manufacturing nation, and then, in order to hinder her from following the impulse thus forcibly given to her, compels her to assist that nation's own colonies to attain independence?

After Huskisson's death, Mr Poulett Thompson undertook the   direction of the commercial affairs of England; this statesman followed his celebrated predecessor in his policy as well as in his office. In the meantime, so far as concerned North America, there remained little for him to do, for in that country, without special efforts on the part of the English, by means of the influence of the cotton planters and the importers, and by the aid of the Democratic party, especially by means of the so-called Compromise Bill in 1832, a modification of the former tariff had taken place, which, although it certainly amended the excesses and faults of the former tariff, and also still secured to the American manufactories a tolerable degree of protection in respect of the coarser fabrics of cotton and woollen, nevertheless gave the English all the concessions which they could have desired without England having been compelled to make any counter concessions.

Since the passing of that Bill, the exports of the English to America have enormously increased. And subsequently to this time they greatly exceed the English imports from North America, so that at any time it is in the power of England to draw to herself as much as she pleases of the precious metals circulating in America, and thereby to occasion commercial crises in the United States as often as she herself is in want of money. But the most astonishing thing in this matter is that that bill had for its author Henry Clay, the most eminent and clearsighted defender of the American manufacturing interest. For it must be remembered that the prosperity of the American manufacturers which resulted from the tariff of 1828 excited so greatly the jealousy of the cotton planters, that the Southern States threatened to bring about a dissolution of the Union in case the tariff of 1828 was not modified. The Federal Government, which was dominated by the Democratic party, had sided with the Southern planters from purely party and electioneering motives, and also managed to get the agriculturists of the Middle and Western States, who belonged to that party, to adopt the same views.

These last had lost their former sympathy with the manufacturing interest in consequence of the high prices of produce which had prevailed, which, however, were the result for the most part of the prosperity of the home manufactories and of the numerous canals and railways which were undertaken. They may also have actually feared that the Southern States would press their opposition so far as to bring about a real dissolution of the Union and even civil war. Hence it became the party interests of the Democrats of the Central and Eastern States not to alienate the sympathies of the Democrats of the Southern States. In consequence of these political circumstances, public opinion veered round so much in favour of free trade with England, that there was reason to fear that all the manufacturing interests of the country might be entirely sacrificed in favour of English free competition. Under such circumstances the Compromise Bill of Henry Clay appeared to be the only means of at least partially preserving the protective system. By this bill part of the American manufactures, viz. those of finer and more expensive articles, was sacrificed to foreign competition, in order to preserve another class of them, viz. the manufacture of articles of a coarser and a less expensive character. In the meantime all appearances seem to indicate that the protective system in North America in the course of the next few years will again raise its head and again make new progress. However much the English may desire to lessen and mitigate the commercial crises in North America, however large also may be the amount of capital which may pass over from England to North America in the form of purchases of stock or of loans or by means of emigration, the existing and still increasing disproportion between the value of the exports and that of imports cannot possibly in the long run be equalised by those means. Alarming commercial crises, which continually increase in their magnitude, must occur, and the Americans must at length be led to recognise the sources of the evil and to determine to put a stop to them.

It thus lies in the very nature of things, that the number of the advocates of the protective system must again increase, and those of free trade again diminish. Hitherto, the prices of agricultural produce have been maintained at an unusually high level, owing to the previous prosperity of the manufactories, through the carrying out of great public undertakings, through the demand for necessaries of life arising from the great increase of the production of cotton, also partially through bad harvests. One may, however, foresee with certainty, that these prices in the course of the next few years will fall as much below the average as they have hitherto ranged above it. The greater part of the increase of American capital has since the passing of the Compromise Bill been devoted to agriculture, and is only now beginning to become productive. While thus agricultural production has unusually increased, on the other hand the demand for it must unusually diminish. Firstly, because public works are no more being undertaken to the same extent; secondly, because the manufacturing population in consequence of foreign competition can no more increase to an important extent; and thirdly, because the production of cotton so greatly exceeds the consumption that the cotton planters will be compelled, owing to the low prices of cotton, to produce for themselves those necessaries of life which they have hitherto procured from the Middle and Western States. If in addition rich harvests occur, then the Middle and Western States will again suffer from an excess of produce, as they did before the tariff of 1828. But the same causes must again produce the same results; viz. the agriculturists of the Middle and Western States must again arrive at the conviction, that the demand for agricultural produce can only be increased by the increase of the manufacturing population of the country, and that that increase can only be brought about by an extension of the protective system. While in this manner the partisans of protection will daily increase in number and influence, the opposite party will diminish in like proportion until the cotton planters under such altered circumstances must necessarily come to the conviction that the increase of the manufacturing population of the country and the increase of the demand for agricultural produce and raw materials both consist with their own interests if rightly understood.

Because, as we have shown, the cotton planters and the Democrats in North America were striving most earnestly of their own accord to play into the hands of the commercial interests of England, no opportunity was offered at the moment on this side for Mr Poulett Thompson to display his skill in commercial diplomacy.

Matters were quite in another position in France. There people still steadily clung to the prohibitive system. There were indeed many State officials who were disciples of theory, and also deputies who were in favour of an extension of commer-

cial relations between England and France, and the existing
alliance with England had also rendered this view to a certain
extent popular. But how to attain that object, opinions were less
agreed, and in no respect were they quite clear. It seemed
evident and also indisputable that the high duties on the foreign
necessaries of life and raw materials, and the exclusion of
English coal and pig-iron, operated very disadvantageously to
French industry, and that an increase in the exports of wines,
brandy, and silk fabrics would be extremely advantageous to
France.

In general, people confined themselves to universal declama-
tion against the disadvantages of the prohibitive system. But to
attack this in special cases did not appear at the time to be at all
advisable. For the Government of July had their strongest
supporters among the rich bourgeoisie, who for the most part
were interested in the great manufacturing undertakings.

Under these circumstances Mr Poulett Thompson formed a
plan of operations which does all honour to his breadth of
thought and diplomatic adroitness. He sent to France a man
thoroughly versed in commerce and industry and in the commercial policy of France, well known for his 'liberal sentiments' a learned man and a very accomplished writer, Dr
Bowring, who travelled through the whole of France, and
subsequently through Switzerland also, to gather on the spot
materials for arguments against the prohibitive system and in
favour of free trade. Dr Bowring accomplished this task with
his accustomed ability and adroitness. Especially he clearly
indicated the before-mentioned advantages of a freer commercial intercourse between the two countries in respect of coal,
pig-iron, wines, and brandies. In the report which he published,
he chiefly confined his arguments to these articles; in reference
to the other branches of industry he only gave statistics, with-

out committing himself to proofs or propositions how these could be promoted by means of free trade with England.

Dr Bowring acted in precise accordance with the instructions given to him by Mr Poulett Thompson, which were framed with uncommon art and subtlety, and which appear at the head of his report. In these Mr Thompson makes use of the most liberal expressions. He expresses himself, with much consideration for the French manufacturing interests, on the improbability that any important result was to be expected from the contemplated negotiations with France. This instruction was perfectly adapted for calming the apprehensions respecting the views of England entertained by the French woollen and cotton manufacturing interests which had become so powerful. According to Mr Thompson, it would be folly to ask for important concessions respecting these.

On the other hand, he gives a hint how the object might more easily be attained in respect of 'less important articles.' These less important articles are certainly not enumerated in the instruction, but the subsequent experience of France has completely brought to light what Mr Thompson meant by it, for at the time of the writing of this instruction the exports of linen yarn and linen fabrics of England to France were included in the term 'less important.'

The French Government, moved by the representations and explanations of the English Government and its agents, and with the intention of making to England a comparatively unimportant concession, which would ultimately prove advantageous to France herself, lowered the duty on linen yarn and linen fabrics to such an extent that they no longer gave any protection to French industry in face of the great improvements which the English had made in these branches of manufacture, so that even in the next few years the export of these articles from England to France increased enormously (1838, 32,000,000 francs); and that France stood in danger, owing to the start which England had thus obtained, of losing its entire linen industry, amounting to many hundred millions in value, which was of the greatest importance for her agriculture and for the welfare of her entire rural population, unless means could be found to put a check on the English competition by increasing the duties.

That France was duped by Mr Poulett Thompson was clear enough. He had already clearly seen in the year 1834 what an impulse the linen manufacture of England would receive in the next few years in consequence of the new inventions which had been made there, and in this negotiation he had calculated on the ignorance of the French Government respecting these inventions and their necessary consequences. The advocates of this lowering of duties now indeed endeavoured to make the world believe that by it they only desired to make a concession to the belgian linen manufactures. But did that make amends for their lack of acquaintance with the advances made by the English, and their lack of foresight as to the necessary consequences?

Be that as it may, this much is clearly demonstrated, that it was necessary for France to protect herself still more, under penalty of losing the greater part of her linen manufacturing for the benefit of England; and that the first and most recent experiment of the increase of freedom of trade between England and France remains as an indelible memorial of English craft and of French inexperience, as a new Methuen Treaty, as a second Eden Treaty. But what did Mr Poulett Thompson do when he perceived the complaints of the French linen manufacturers and the inclination of the French Government to repair the mistake which had been made? He did what Mr Huskisson had done before him, he indulged in threats, he threatened to exclude French wines and silk fabrics. This is English cosmopolitanism. France must give up a manufacturing industry of a thousand years' standing, bound up in the closest manner with the entire economy of her lower classes and especially with her agriculture, the products of which must be reckoned as chief necessaries of life for all classes, and of the entire amount of between three and four hundred millions, in order thereby to purchase the privilege of exporting to England some few millions more in value of wines and silk manufactures. Quite apart from this disproportion in value, it must be considered in what a position France would be placed if the commercial relations between both nations became interrupted in consequence of a war; in case viz. that France could no more export to England her surplus products of silk manufactures and wines, but at the same time suffered from the want of such an important necessary of life as linen.

If anyone reflects on this he will see that the linen question is not simply a question of economical well-being, but, as everything is which concerns the national manufacturing power, is still more a question of the independence and power of the nation.

It seems indeed as if the spirit of invention had set itself the task, in this perfecting of the linen manufacture, to make the nations comprehend the nature of the manufacturing interest, its relations with agriculture, and its influence on the independence and power of the State, and to expose the erroneous arguments of the popular theory. The school maintains, as is well known, that every nation possesses special advantages in various branches of production, which she has either derived from nature, or which she has partly acquired in the course of her career, and which under free trade compensate one another.

We have in a previous chapter adduced proof that this argument is only true in reference to agriculture, in which production depends for the most part on climate and on the fertility of the soil, but that it is not true in respect to manufacturing industry, for which all nations inhabiting temperate climates have equal capability provided that they possess the necessary material, mental, social, and political qualifications. England at the present day offers the most striking proof of this. If any nations whatever are specially adapted by their past experience and exertions, and through their natural qualifications, for the manufacture of linen, those are the Germans, the belgians, the Dutch, and the inhabitants of the North of France for a thousand years past. The English, on the other hand, up to the middle of the last century, had notoriously made such small progress in that industry, that they imported a great proportion of the linen which they required, from abroad. It would never have been possible for them, without the duties by which they continuously protected this manufacturing industry, even to supply their own markets and colonies with linen of their own manufacture. And it is well known how Lords Castlereagh and Liverpool adduced proof in Parliament, that without protection it was impossible for the Irish linen manufactures to sustain competition with those of Germany. At present, however, we see how the English threaten to monopolise the linen manufacture of the whole of Europe, in consequence of their inventions, notwithstanding that they were for a hundred years the worst manufacturers of linen in all Europe, just as they have monopolised for the last fifty years the cotton markets of the East Indies, notwithstanding that one hundred years previously they could not even compete in their own market with the Indian cotton manufacturers. At this moment it is a matter of dispute in France how it happens that England has lately made such immense progress in the manufacture of linen, although Napoleon was the first who offered such a great reward for the invention of a machine for spinning cotton, and that the French machinists and manufacturers had been engaged in this trade before the English. The inquiry is made whether the English or the French possessed more mechanical talent. All kinds of explanations are offered except the true and the natural one. It is absurd to attribute specially to the English greater mechanical talent, or greater skill and perseverance in industry, than to the Germans or to the French. Before the time of Edward III the English were the greatest bullies and good-for-nothing characters in Europe; certainly it never occurred to them to compare themselves with the Italians and Belgians or with the Germans in respect to mechanical talent or industrial skill; but since then their Government has taken their education in hand, and thus they have by degrees made such progress that they can dispute the palm of industrial skill with their instructors. If the English in the last twenty years have made more rapid progress in machinery for linen manufacture than other nations, and especially the French, have done, this has only occurred because, firstly, they had attained greater eminence in mechanical skill; secondly, that they were further advanced in machinery for spinning and weaving cotton, which is so similar to that for spinning and weaving linen; thirdly, that in consequence of their previous commercial policy, they had become possessed of more capital than the French; fourthly, that in consequence of that commercial policy their home market for linen goods was far more extensive than that of the French; and lastly that their protective duties, combined with the circumstances above named, afforded to the mechanical talent of the nation greater stimulus and more means to devote itself to perfecting this branch of industry.

The English have thus given a striking confirmation of the opinions which we in another place have propounded and explained —that all individual branches of industry have the closest reciprocal effect on one another; that the perfecting of one branch prepares and promotes the perfecting of all others; that no one of them can be neglected without the effects of that neglect being felt by all; that, in short, the whole manufacturing power of a nation constitutes an inseparable whole. Of these opinions they have by their latest achievements in the linen industry offered a striking confirmation.

NOTES:

1. Even a part of the production of wool in England is due to the observance of this maxim. Edward IV imported under special privileges 3,000 head of sheep from Spain (where the export of sheep was prohibited), and distributed them among various parishes, with a command that for seven years none were to be slaughtered or castrated. (Essai sur le Commerce d'Angleterre, tome i. p. 379.) As soon as the object of these measures had been attained, England rewarded the Spanish Government for the special privileges granted by the latter, by prohibiting the import of Spanish wool. The efficacy of this prohibition (however unjust it may be deemed) can as little be denied as that of the prohibitions of the import of wool by Charles II (1672 and 1674).

2. France, said Pitt, has advantages above England in respect of climate and other natural gifts, and therefore excels England in its raw produce; on the other hand, England has the advantage over France in its artificial products. The wines, brandies, oils, and vinegars of France, especially the first two, articles of such

importance and of such value, that the value of our natural products cannot be in the least compared with them. But, on the other hand, it is equally certain that England is the exclusive producer of some kinds of manufactured goods, and that in respect of other kinds she possesses such advantages that she can defy without doubt all the competition of France. This is a reciprocal condition and a basis on which an advantageous commercial treaty between both nations should be founded. As each of them has its peculiar staple commodities, and each possesses that which is lacking to the other, so both should deal with one another like two great merchants who are engaged in different branches of trade, and by a reciprocal exchange of their goods can at once become useful to one another. Let us further only call to mind on this point the wealth of the county with which we stand in the position of neighbours, its great population, its vicinity to us, and the consequent quick and regular exchange. Who could then hesitate a moment to give his approval to the system of freedom, and who would not earnestly and impatiently wish for the utmost possible expedition in establishing it? The possession of such an extensive and certain market must give quite an extraordinary impulse to our trade, and the customs revenue which would then be diverted from the hands of the smuggler into the State revenue would benefit our finances, and thus two main springs of British wealth and of British power would be made more productive.

3. Since List wrote these lines, the duties which foreign silk manufacturers had to pay on the import of their goods into England have been totally abolished. The results of their abolition may be learned from Mr Wardle's report on the English silk trade, as follows: London, in 1825, contained 24,000 looms and 60,000 operatives engaged in silk manufac-

ture. At the present time these have dwindled to 1,200 looms and less then 4,000 operatives. In Coventry, in 1861, the ribbon trade is stated to have given subsistence to 40,600 persons; while at the present time probably not more than 10,000 persons are supported by it, and the power-looms at work in Coventry have decreased from 1,800 to 600. In Derby the number of operatives employed in silk manufacture has decreased from 6,650 (in 1850) to 2,400 at present. In the Congleton district they have decreased from 5,186 (in 1860) to 1,530 (in 1884); while of the forty silk-throwsters' works which that district contained (in 1859) only twelve now remain, with 'about three-fourths of their machinery employed.' In Manchester this trade has practically died out, while at Middleton the industry is 'simply ruined.' These results (stated by Mr Wardle) may account for the decrease in England's imports of raw silk, from 8,000,000 pounds (in 1871) to less than 3,000,000 pounds.

On the other hand, since List wrote, the United States of America have increased and steadily maintained a considerable protective duty on the importation of foreign silk manufactures. The results of that policy were publicly stated by Mr Robert P. Porter (member of the United States' Tariff Commission), in a speech in 1883, to have been as follows:

Five thousand persons were employed in silk manufacture in the United States before the Morill tariff (1861). In 1880 their number had increased to 30,000. The value of silk manufactures produced in the States increased from 1,200,000 l. in 1860 to more than 8,000,000 l. in 1880. 'Yet the cost of the manufactured goods to the consumer, estimated on a gold basis, has steadily declined at a much greater rate than the cost of the raw material.' After reference to the earthenware and plate-glass manufactures, Mr Porter adds: 'The testimony before the Tariff Commission showed unquestionably that the competition in the United States had resulted in a reduction in the cost to the American consumer. In this way, gentlemen, I contend, and am prepared to prove statistically. that protection, so far as the United States are concerned, has in every case ultimately benefited the consumer; and on this ground I defend it and believe in it.' — TRANSLATOR.

4. Chaptal, De l'Industrie Française vol. ii., p. 147.

Chapter 34

The Insular Supremacy and the German Commercial Union

What a great nation is at the present day without a vigorous commercial policy, and what she may become by the adoption of a vigorous commercial policy, Germany has learnt for herself during the last twenty years. Germany was that which Franklin once said of the State of New Jersey, 'a cask which was tapped and drained by its neighbours on every side.' England, not contented with having ruined for the Germans the greater part of their own manufactories and supplied them with enormous quantities of cotton and woollen fabrics, excluded from her ports German grain and timber, nay from time to time also even German wool. There was a time when the export of manufactured goods from England to Germany was ten times greater than that to her highly extolled East Indian Empire. Nevertheless the all-monopolising islanders would not even grant to the poor Germans what they conceded to the con- quered Hindoos, viz. to pay for the manufactured goods which they required by agricultural produce. In vain did the Germans humble themselves to the position of hewers of wood and drawers of water for the Britons. The latter treated them worse than a subject people. Nations, like individuals, if they at first only permit themselves to be ill-treated by one, soon become scorned by all, and finally become an object of derision to the very children. France, not contented with exporting to Germany enormous quantities of wine, oil, silk, and millinery, grudged the Germans their exports of cattle, grain, and flax; yes, even a small maritime province formerly possessed by Germany and inhabited by Germans, which having become wealthy and powerful by means of Germany, at all times was only able to maintain itself with and by means of Germany, barred for half a generation Germany's greatest river by means of contemptible verbal quibbles. To fill up the measure of this contempt, the doctrine was taught from a hundred professorial chairs, that nations could only attain to wealth and power by means of universal free trade. Thus it was; but how is it now? Germany has advanced in prosperity and industry, in national self-respect and in national power, in the course of ten years as much as in a century. And how has this result been achieved? It was certainly good and beneficial that the internal tariffs were abolished which separated Germans from Germans; but the nation would have derived small comfort from that if her home industry had thenceforth remained freely exposed to foreign competition. It was especially the protection which the tariff of the Zollverein secured to manufactured articles of common use, which has wrought this miracle. Let us freely confess it, for Dr Bowring(1*) has incontrovertibly shown it, that the Zollverein tariff has not, as was before asserted, imposed merely duties for revenue — that it has not confined itself to duties of ten to fifteen per cent as Huskisson believed — let us freely admit that it has imposed protective duties of from twenty to sixty per cent as respects the manufactured articles of common use.

But what has been the operation of these protective duties? Are the consumers paying for their German manufactured goods twenty to sixty per cent more than they formerly paid for foreign ones (as must be the case if the popular theory is correct), or are these goods at all worse than the foreign ones? Nothing of the sort. Dr Bowring himself adduces testimony that the manufactured goods produced under the high customs tariff are both better and cheaper than the foreign ones.(2*) The internal competition and the security from destructive competition by the foreigner has wrought this miracle, of which the popular school knows nothing and is determined to know nothing. Thus, that is not true, which the popular school maintains, that a protective duty increases the price of the goods of home production by the amount of the protective duty. For a short time the duty may increase the price, but in every nation which is qualified to carry on manufacturing industry the consequence of the protection will be, that the internal competition will soon reduce the prices lower than they had stood at when the importation was free.

But has agriculture at all suffered under these high duties? Not in the least; it has gained-gained tenfold during the last ten years. The demand for agricultural produce has increased. The prices of it everywhere are higher. It is notorious that solely in consequence of the growth of the home manufactories the value of land has everywhere risen from fifty to a hundred per cent, that everywhere higher wages are being paid, and that in all directions improvements in the means of transport are either being effected or projected.

Such brilliant results as these must necessarily encourage us to proceed farther on the system which we have commenced to follow. Other States of the Union have also proposed to take similar steps, but have not yet carried them into effect; while, as it would appear, some other States of the Union only expect to attain prosperity solely by the abolition of the English duties on grain and timber, and while (as it is alleged) there are still to be found influential men who believe in the cosmopolitical system and distrust their own experience. Dr Bowring's report gives us most important explanations on these points as well as on the circumstances of the German Commercial Union and the tactics of the English Government. Let us endeavour to throw a little light on this report.

First of all, we have to consider the point of view from which it was written. Mr Labouchere, President of the board of Trade under the Melbourne Ministry, had sent Dr Bowring to Germany for the same purpose as that for which Mr Poulett Thompson had sent him to France in the year 1834. Just as it was intended to mislead the French by concessions in respect of wines and brandies to open their home market to English manufactured goods, so it was intended to mislead the Germans to do the same by concessions in respect of grain and timber; only there was a great difference between the two missions in this respect, that the concession which was to be offered to the French had to fear no opposition in England, while that which had to be offered to the Germans had first to be fought for in England herself.

Hence the tendency of these two reports was of necessity of quite a different character. The report on the commercial relations between France and England was written exclusively for the French; to them it was necessary to represent that Colbert had accomplished nothing satisfactory through his protective regulations; it was necessary to make people believe that the Eden Treaty was beneficial to France, and that Napoleon's Continental system, as well as the then existing French prohibitive system, had been extremely injurious to her. In short, in this case it was necessary to stick closely to the theory of Adam Smith; and the good results of the protective system must be completely and unequivocally denied. The task was not quite so simple with the other report, for in this, one had to address the English land-owners and the German Governments at one and the same time. To the former it was necessary to say: See, there is a nation which has already in consequence of protective regulations made enormous advances in her industry, and which, in possession of all necessary means for doing so, is making rapid steps to monopolise her own home market and to compete with England in foreign markets. This, you Tories in the House of Lords — this, you country squires in the House of Commons, is your wicked doing. This has been brought about by your unwise corn laws; for by them the prices of provisions and raw materials and the wages of labour have been kept low in Germany. By them the German manufactories have been placed in an advantageous position compared to the English ones. Make haste, therefore, you fools, to abolish these corn laws. By that means you will doubly and trebly damage the German manufactories : firstly, because the prices of provisions and raw materials and the wages of labour will be raised in Germany and lowered in England; secondly, because by the export of German grain to England the export of English manufactured goods to Germany will be promoted; thirdly, because the German Commercial Union has declared that it is disposed to reduce their duties on common cotton and woollen goods in the same proportion in which England facilitates the import of German grain and timber. Thus we Britons cannot fail once more to crush the German manufactories. But the question cannot wait. Every year the manufacturing interests are gaining greater influence in the German Union; and if you delay, then your corn-law abolition will come too late. It will not be long before the balance will turn. Very soon the German manufactories will create such a great demand for agricultural produce that Germany will have no more surplus corn to sell to foreign countries. What concessions, then, are you willing to offer to the German Governments to induce them to lay hands on their own manufactories in order to hinder them from spinning cotton for themselves, and from encroaching upon your foreign markets in addition?

All this the writer of the report was compelled to make clear to the landowners in Parliament. The forms of the British State administration permit no secret Government reports. Dr Bowring's report must be published, must therefore be seen by the Germans in translations and extracts. Hence one must use no expressions which might lead the Germans to a perception of their true interests. Therefore to every method which was adapted to influence Parliament, an antidote must be added for the use of the German Governments. It must be alleged, that in consequence of the protective system much German capital had been diverted into improper channels. The agricultural interests of Germany would be damaged by the protective system. That interest for its part ought only to turn its attention to foreign markets; agriculture was in Germany by far the most important productive industry, for three-fourths of the inhabitants of Germany were engaged in it. It was mere nonsense to talk about protection for the producers; the manufacturing interest itself could only thrive under foreign competition : public opinion in Germany desired freedom of trade. Intelligence in Germany was too universal for a desire for high duties to be entertained. The most enlightened men in the country were in favour of a reduction of duties on common woollen and cotton fabrics, in case the English duties on corn and timber were reduced.

In short, in this report two entirely different voices speak, which contradict one another like two opponents. Which of the two must be deemed the true one-that which speaks to the Parliament, or that which speaks to the German Governments? There is no difficulty in deciding this point, for everything which Dr Bowring adduces in order to induce Parliament to lower the import duties on grain and timber is supported by statistical facts, calculations, and evidence; while everything that he adduces to dissuade the German Governments from the protective system is confined to mere superficial assertions.

Let us consider in detail the arguments by which Dr Bowring proves to the Parliament that in case a check is not put to the progress of the German protective system in the way which he pointed out, the German market for manufactured goods must become irrecoverably lost to England.

The German people is remarkable, says Dr Bowring, for temperance, thrift, industry, and intelligence, and enjoys a system of universal education. Excellent polytechnic schools diffuse technical instruction throughout the entire country.

The art of design is especially much more cultivated there than in England. The great annual increase of its population, of its head of cattle, and especially of sheep, proves what progress agriculture there has achieved. (The report makes no mention of the improvement in the value of property, though that is an important feature, nor of the increase in the value of produce.) The wages of labour have risen thirty per cent in the manufacturing districts. The country possesses a great amount of water power, as yet unused, which is the cheapest of all motive powers. Its mining industry is everywhere flourishing, more than at any previous time. From 1832 up to 1837 the imports of raw cotton have increased from 118,000 centners to 240,000 centners; the imports of cotton yarn from 172,000 centners to 322,000 centners; the exports of cotton fabrics from 26,000 centners to 75,000 centners; the number of cotton-weaving looms in Prussia from 22,000 in 1825 to 32,000 in 1834; the imports of raw wool from 99,000 centners to 195,000 centners; the exports of the same from 100,000 centners to 122,000 centners; the imports of woollen articles from 15,000 centners to 18,000 centners; the exports of the same from 49,000 centners to 69,000 centners.

The manufacture of linen cloths contends with difficulty against the high duties in England, France, and Italy and has not increased. On the other hand, the imports of linen yarn have increased from 30,000 centners in 1832 to 86,000 centners in 1835, chiefly through the imports from England, which are still increasing. The consumption of indigo increased from 12,000 centners in 1831 to 24,000 centners in 1837; a striking proof of the progress of German industry. The exports of pottery have been more than doubled from 1832 to 1836. The imports of stoneware have diminished from 5,000 centners to 2,000 centners, and the exports of it increased from 4,000 centners to 18,000 centners. The imports of porcelain have diminished from 4,000 centners to 1,000 centners, and the exports of it have increased from 700 centners to 4,000 centners. The output of coal has increased from 6,000,000 Prussian tons in 1832 to 9,000,000 in 1836. In 1816 there were 8,000,000 sheep in Prussia; and in 1837, 15,000,000.

In Saxony in 1831 there were 14,000 stocking-weaving machines; in 2836, 20,000. From 1831 to 1837, the number of manufactories for spinning woollen yarn and of spindles had increased in Saxony to more than double their previous number. Everywhere machine manufactories had arisen, and many of these were in the most flourishing condition.

In short, in all branches of industry, in proportion as they have been protected, Germany has made enormous advances, especially in woollen and cotton goods for common use, the importation of which from England had entirely ceased. At the same time Dr Bowring admits, in consequence of a trustworthy opinion which had been expressed to him, 'that the price of the Prussian stuffs was decidedly lower than that of the English; that certainly in respect of some of the colours they were inferior to the best English tints, but that others were perfect and could not be surpassed; that in spinning, weaving, and all preparatory processes, the German goods were fully equal to the British, but only in the finish a distinct inferiority might be observed, but that the want of this would disappear after a little time.'

It is very easy to understand how by means of such representations as these the English Parliament may at length be induced to abandon its corn laws, which have hitherto operated as a protective system to Germany. But it appears to us utterly incomprehensible how the German Union, which has made such enormous advances in consequence of the protective system, should be induced by this report to depart from a system which has yielded them such excellent results.

It is very well for Dr Bowring to assure us that the home industry of Germany is being protected at the expense of the agriculturists. But how can we attach any credence to his assurance, when we see, on the contrary, that the demand for agricultural produce, prices of produce, the wages of labour, the rents, the value of property, have everywhere considerably risen, without the agriculturist having to pay more than he did before for the manufactured goods which he requires?

It is very well for Dr Bowring to give us an estimate showing that in Germany three persons are engaged in agriculture to every one in manufactures, but that statement convinces us that the number of Germans engaged in manufacturing is not yet in proper proportion to the number of German agriculturists. And we cannot see by what other means this disproportion can be equalised, than by increasing the protection on those branches of manufacture which are still carried on in England for the supply of the German market by persons who consume English instead of German agricultural produce. It is all very well for

Dr Bowring to assert that German agriculture must only direct its attention to foreign countries if it desires to increase its sale of produce; but that a great demand for agricultural produce can only be attained by a flourishing home manufacturing power is taught us not alone by the experience of England, but Dr Bowring himself implicitly admits this, by the apprehension which he expresses in his report, that if England delays for some time to abolish her corn laws, Germany will then have no surplus of either corn or timber to sell to foreign countries.

Dr Bowring is certainly right when he asserts that the agricultural interest in Germany is still the predominant one, but just for the very reason that it is predominant it must (as we have shown in former chapters), by promoting the manufacturing interests, seek to place itself in a just proportion with them, because the prosperity of agriculture depends on its being in equal proportion with the manufacturing interest, but not on its own preponderance over it.

Further, the author of the report appears to be utterly steeped in error when he maintains that foreign competition in German markets is necessary for the German manufacturing interest itself, because the German manufacturers, as soon as they are in a position to supply the German markets, must compete with the manufacturers of other countries for the disposal of their surplus produce, which competition they can only sustain by means of cheap production. But cheap production will not consist with the existence of the protective system, inasmuch as the object of that system is to secure higher prices to the manufacturers.

This argument contains as many errors and falsehoods as words. Dr Bowring cannot deny that the manufacturer can offer his products at cheaper prices, the more he is enabled to manufacture — that, therefore, a manufacturing Power which exclusively possesses its home market can work so much the cheaper for foreign trade. The proof of this he can find in the same tables which he has published on the advances made by German industry; for in the same proportion in which the German manufactories have acquired possession of their own home market, their export of manufactured goods has also increased. Thus the recent experience of Germany, like the ancient experience of England, shows us that high prices of manufactured goods are by no means a necessary consequence of protection.

Finally, German industry is still very far from entirely supplying her home market. In order to do that, she must first manufacture for herself the 13,000 centners of cotton fabrics, the 18,000 centners of woollen fabrics, the 500,000 centners of cotton yarn, thread, and linen yarn, which at present are imported from England. If, however, she accomplishes that, she will then import 500,000 centners more raw cotton than before, by which she will carry on so much the more direct exchange trade with tropical countries, and be able to pay for the greater part if not the whole of that requirement with her own manufactured goods.

We must correct the view of the author of the report, that public opinion in Germany is in favour of free trade, by stating that since the establishment of the Commercial Union people have acquired a clearer perception of what it is that England usually understands by the term 'free trade,' for, as he himself says, 'Since that period the sentiments of the German people have been diverted from the region of hope and of fantasy to that of their actual and material interests.' The author of the report is quite right when he says that intelligence is very greatly diffused amongst the German people, but for that very reason people in Germany have ceased to indulge in cosmopolitical dreams. People here now think for themselves — they trust their own conclusions, their own experience, their own sound common sense, more than one-sided systems which are opposed to all experience. They begin to comprehend why it was that Burke declared in confidence to Adam Smith 'that a nation must not be governed according to cosmopolitical systems, but according to knowledge of their special national interests acquired by deep research.' People in Germany distrust counsellors who blow both cold and hot out of the same mouth. People know also how to estimate at their proper value the interests and the advice of those who are our industrial competitors. Finally, people in Germany bear in mind as often as English offers are under discussion the well-known proverb of the presents offered by the Danaidae.

For these very reasons we may doubt that influential German statesmen have seriously given grounds for hope to the author of the report, that Germany is willing to abandon her protective policy for the benefit of England, in exchange for the pitiful concession of permission to export to England a little grain and timber. At any rate public opinion in Germany would greatly hesitate to consider such statesmen to be thoughtful ones. In order to merit that title in Germany in the present day, it is not enough that a man should have thoroughly learned superficial phrases and arguments of the cosmopolitical school. People require that a statesman should be well acquainted with the powers and the requirements of the nation, and, without troubling himself with scholastic systems, should develop the former and satisfy the latter. But that man would betray an unfathomable ignorance of those powers and wants, who did not know what enormous exertions are requisite to raise a national industry to that stage to which the German industry has already attained; who cannot in spirit foresee the greatness of its future; who could so grievously disappoint the confidence which the German industrial classes have reposed in their Governments, and so deeply wound the spirit of enterprise in the nation; who was incapable of distinguishing between the lofty position which is occupied by a manufacturing nation of the first rank, and the inferior position of a country which merely exports corn and timber; who is not intelligent enough to estimate how precarious a foreign market for grain and timber is even in ordinary times, how easily concessions of this kind can be again revoked, and what convulsions are involved in an interruption of such a trade, occasioned by wars or hostile commercial regulations; who, finally, has not learned from the example of other great states how greatly the existence, the independence, and the power of the nation depends on its possession of a manufacturing power of its own, developed in all its branches.

Truly one must greatly under-estimate the spirit of nationalitya and of unity which has arisen in Germany since 1830, if one believed, as the author of the report does (p. 26), that the policy of the Commercial Union will follow the separate interests of Prussia, because two-thirds of the population of the Union are Prussian. But Prussia's interests demand the export of grain and timber to England; the amount of her capital devoted to manufactures is unimportant; Prussia will therefore oppose every system which impedes the import of foreign manufactures, and all the heads of departments in Prussia are of that opinion. Nevertheless the author of the report says at the beginning of his report: 'The German Customs Union is an incarnation of the idea of national unity which widely pervades this country. If this Union is well led, it must bring about the fusion of all German interests in one common league. The experience of its benefits has made it popular. It is the first step towards the nationalisation of the German people. By means of the common interest in commercial questions, it has paved the way for political nationality, and in place of narrow-minded views, prejudices, and customs, it has laid down a broader and stronger element of German national existence.' Now, how does the opinion agree with these perfectly true prefatory observations, that Prussia will sacrifice the independence and the future greatness of the nation to a narrow regard to her own supposed (but in any case only momentary) private interest — that Prussia will not comprehend that Germany must either rise or fall with her national commercial policy, as Prussia herself must rise or fall with Germany? How does the assertion that the Prussian heads of departments are opposed to the protective system, agree with the fact that the high duties on ordinary woollen and cotton fabrics emanated from Prussia herself? And must we not be compelled to conjecture from these contradictions, and from the fact that the author of the report paints in such glowing colours the condition and the progress of the industry of Saxony, that he himself is desirous of exciting the private jealousy of Prussia?

Be that as it may, it is very strange that Dr Bowring attaches such great importance to the private statements of heads of departments, he an English author who ought to be well aware of the power of public opinion — who ought to know that in our days the private views of heads of departments even in unconstitutional states count for very little if they are opposed to public opinion, and especially to the material interests of the whole nation, and if they favour retrograde steps which endanger the whole nationality. The author of the report also feels this well enough himself, when he states at page 98 that the Prussian Government has sufficiently experienced, as the

English Government has done in connection with the abolition of the English corn laws, that the views of public officials cannot everywhere be carried into effect, that hence it might be necessary to consider whether German grain and timber should not be admitted to the English markets even without previous concessions on the part of the German Union, because by that very means the way might be paved for the admission of the English manufactured goods into the German market. This view is in any case a correct one. Dr Bowring sees clearly that the German industry would never have been strengthened but for those laws; that consequently the abolition of the corn laws would not only check the further advances of German industry, but must cause it again to retrograde greatly, provided always that in that case the German customs legislation remains unchanged. It is only a pity that the British did not perceive the soundness of this argument twenty years ago; but now, after that the legislation of England has itself undertaken the divorce of German agriculture from English manufactures, after that Germany has pursued the path of perfecting her industry for twenty years, and has made enormous sacrifices for this object, it would betoken political blindness if Germany were now, owing to the abolition of the English corn laws, to abstain in any degree from pursuing her great national career. Indeed, we are firmly convinced that in such a case it would be necessary for Germany to increase her protective duties in the same proportion in which the English manufactories would derive advantage from the abolition of the corn laws as compared with those of Germany. Germany can for a long time follow no other policy in respect to England than that of a less advanced manu-facturing nation which is striving with all her power to raise herself to an equal position with the most advanced manufac-turing nation. Every other policy or measure than that, involves the imperilling of the German nationality. If the English are in want of foreign corn or timber, then they may get it in Germany or where else they please. Germany will not on that account any the less protect the advances in industry which she has made up to this time, or strive any the less to make future advances. If the British will have nothing to do with German grain and timber, so much the better. In that case the industry, the navigation, the foreign trade of Germany will raise their heads so much the quicker, the German internal means of transport will be so much the sooner completed, the German nationality will so much the more certainly rest on its natural foundation. Perhaps Prussia may not in this way so soon be able to sell the corn and timber of her Baltic provinces at high prices as if the English markets were suddenly opened to her. But through the completion of the internal means of transport, and through the internal demand for agricultural produce created by the manufactories, the sales of those provinces to the interior of Germany will increase fast enough, and every benefit to these provinces which is founded on the home demand for agricultural produce will be gained by them for all future time. They will never more have to oscillate as heretofore between calamity and prosperity from one decade to another. But further, as a political power Prussia will gain a hundred-fold more in concentrated strength in the interior of Germany by this policy than the material values which she sacrifices for the moment in her maritime provinces, or rather invests for repayment in the future.

The object of the English ministry in this report is clearly to obtain the admission into Germany of ordinary English woollen and cotton fabrics, partly through the abolition or at least modification of charging duties by weight, partly through the lowering of the tariff, and partly by the admission of the German grain and timber into the English market. By these means the first breach can be made in the German protective system. These articles of ordinary use (as we have already shown in a former chapter) are by far the most important, they are the fundamental element of the national industry. Duties of ten per cent ad valorem, which are clearly aimed at by England, would, with the assistance of the usual tricks of under declaration of value, sacrifice the greater part of the German industry to English competition, especially if in consequence of commercial crises the English manufacturers were sometimes induced to throw on the market their stocks of goods at any price. It is therefore no exaggeration if we maintain that the tendency of the English proposals aims at nothing less than the overthrow of the entire German protective system, in order to reduce Germany to the position of an English agricultural colony. With this object in view it is impressed on.the notice of Prussia how greatly her agriculture might gain by the reduction of the English corn and timber duties, and how unimportant her manufacturing interest is. With the same view, the prospect is offered to Prussia of a reduction of the duties on brandy. And in order that the other states may not go quite empty away a five per cent reduction of the duties on Nüremberg wares, children's toys, eau de Cologne, and other trifles, is promised. That gives satisfaction to the small German states, and also does not cost much.

The next attempt will be to convince the German governments, by means of this report, how advantageous to them it would be to let England spin cotton and linen yarns for them. It cannot be doubted that hitherto the policy adopted by the Union, first of all to encourage and protect the printing of cloths and then weaving, and to import the medium and finer yarns, has been the right one. But from that it in nowise follows that it would continue to be the right one for all time. The tariff legislation must advance as the national industry advances if it is rightly to fulfil its purpose. We have already shown that the spinning factories, quite apart from their importance in themselves, yet are the source of further incalculable benefits, inasmuch as they place us in direct commercial communication with the countries of warm climate, and hence that they exercise an incalculable influence on our navigation and on our export of manufactures, and that they benefit our manufactories of machinery more than any other branch of manufacture. Inasmuch as it cannot be doubted that Germany cannot be hindered either by want of water power and of capable workmen, or by lack of material capital or intelligence, from carrying on for herself this great and fruitful industry, so we cannot see why we should not gradually protect the spinning of yarns from one number to another, in such a way that in the course of five to ten years we may be able to spin for ourselves the greater part of what we require. However highly one may estimate the advantages of the export of grain and timber, they cannot nearly equal the benefits which must accrue to us from the spinning manufacture. Indeed, we have no hesitation in expressing the belief that it could be incontestably proved, by a calculation of the consumption of agricultural products and timber which would be created by the spinning industry, that from this branch of manufacture alone far greater benefits must accrue to the German landowners than the foreign market will ever or can ever offer them.

Dr Bowring doubts that Hanover, Brunswick, the two Mecklenburgs, Oldenburg, and the Hanse Towns will join the Union, unless the latter is willing to make a radical reduction in its import duties. The latter proposal, however, cannot be seriously considered, because it would be immeasurably worse than the evil which by it, it is desired to remedy.

Our confidence in the prosperity of the future of Germany is, however, by no means so weak as that of the author of the report. Just as the Revolution of July has proved beneficial to the German Commercial Union, so must the next great general convulsion make an end of all the minor hesitations by which these small states have hitherto been withheld from yielding to the greater requirements of the German nationality. Of what value the commercial unity has been to the nationality, and of what value it is to German governments, quite apart from mere material interests, has been recently for the first time very strongly demonstrated, when the desire to acquire the Rhine frontier has been loudly expressed in France.

From day to day it is necessary that the governments and peoples of Germany should be more convinced that national unity is the rock on which the edifice of their welfare, their honour, their power, their present security and existence, and their future greatness, must be founded. Thus from day to day the apostasy of these small maritime states will appear more and more, not only to the states in the Union, but to these small states themselves, in the light of a national scandal which must be got rid of at any price. Also, if the matter is intelligently considered, the material advantages of joining the Union are much greater for those states themselves than the sacrifice which it requires. The more that manufacturing industry, that the internal means of transport, the navigation, and the foreign trade of Germany, develop themselves, in that degree in which under a wise commercial policy they can and must be developed in accordance with the resources of the nation, so much the more will the desire become more vigorous on the part of those small states directly to participate in these advantages, and so much the more will they leave off the bad habit of looking to foreign countries for blessings and prosperity.

In reference to the Hanse Towns especially, the spirit of imperial citizenship of the sovereign parish of Hamburg in no way deters us from our hopes. In those cities, according to the testimony of the author of the report himself, dwell a great number of men who comprehend that Hamburg, Bremen, and Lubeck are and must be to the German nation that which London and Liverpool are to the English, that which New York, Boston, and Philadelphia are to the Americans — men who clearly see that the Commercial Union can offer advantages to their commerce with the world which far exceed the disadvantages of subjection to the regulations of the Union, and that a prosperity without any guarantee for its continuance is fundamentally a delusion.

What sensible inhabitant of those seaports could heartily congratulate himself on the continual increase of their tonnage, on the continual extension of their commercial relations, if he reflected that two frigates, which coming from Heligoland could be stationed at the mouths of the Weser and the Elbe, would be in a position to destroy in twenty-four hours this work of a quarter of a century? But the Union will guarantee to these seaports their prosperity and their progress for all future time, partly by the creation of a fleet of its own and partly by alliances. It will foster their fisheries, secure special advantages to their shipping, protect and promote their foreign commercial relations, by effective consular establishments and by treaties. Partly by their means it will found new colonies, and by their means carry on its own colonial trade. For a union of States comprising thirty-five millions of inhabitants (for the Union will comprise that number at least when it is fully completed), which owing to an annual increase of population of one and a half per cent can easily spare annually two or three hundred thousand persons, whose provinces abound with well-informed and cultivated inhabitants who have a peculiar propensity to seek their fortune in distant countries, people who can take root anywhere and make themselves at home wherever unoccupied land is to be cultivated, are called upon by Nature herself to place themselves in the first rank of nations who colonise and diffuse civilisation.

The feeling of the necessity for such a perfect completion of the Commercial Union is so universally entertained in Germany, that hence the author of the report could not help remarking, 'More coasts, more harbours, more navigation, a Union flag, the possession of a navy and of a mercantile marine, are wishes very generally entertained by the supporters of the Commercial Union, but there is little prospect at present of the Union making head against the increasing fleet of Russia and the commercial marine of Holland and the Hanse Towns.' Against them certainly not, but so much the more with them and by means of them. It lies in the very nature of every power to seek to divide in order to rule. After the author of the report has shown why it would be foolish on the part of the maritime states to join the Union, he desires also to separate the great seaports from the German national body for all time, inasmuch as he speaks to us of the warehouses of Altona which must become dangerous to the warehouses of Hamburg, as though such a great commercial empire could not find the means of making the warehouses of Altona serviceable to its objects. We will not follow the author through his acute inferences from this point; we will only say, that if they were applied to England, they would prove that London and Liverpool would increase their commercial prosperity in an extraordinary degree if they were separated from the body of the English nation. The spirit which underlies these arguments is unmistakably expressed in the report of the English consul at Rotterdam. 'For the commercial interests of Great Britain,' says Mr Alexander Ferrier at the end of his report, 'it appears of the greatest possible importance that no means should be left untried to prevent the aforesaid states, and also Belgium, from entering the Zollverein, for reasons which are too clear to need any exposition.' Who could possibly blame Mr Ferrier for speaking thus, or Dr Bowring for speaking thus, or the English ministers for acting as the others speak? The national instinct of England speaks and acts through them. But to expect prosperity and blessing to Germany from proposals which proceed from such a source as that, would appear to exceed even a decent degree of national good nature. 'Whatever may happen,' adds Mr Ferrier to the words above quoted, 'Holland must at all times be considered as the main channel for the commercial relations of South Germany with other countries.' Clearly Mr Ferrier understands by the term 'other countries' merely England; clearly he means to say that if the English manufacturing supremacy should lose its means of access to Germany or the North Sea and the Baltic, Holland would still remain to it as the great means of access by which it could predominate over the markets for manufactured goods and colonial produce of the south of Germany.

But we from a national point of view say and maintain that Holland is in reference to its geographical position, as well as in respect to its commercial and industrial circumstances, and to the origin and language of its inhabitants, a German province, which has been separated from Germany at a period of German national disunion, without whose reincorporation in the German Union Germany may be compared to a house the door of which belongs to a stranger: Holland belongs as much to Germany as Brittany and Normandy belong to France, and so long as Holland is determined to constitute an independent kingdom of her own, Germany can as little attain independence and power as France would have been enabled to attain these if those provinces had remained in the hands of the English. That the commercial power of Holland has declined, is owing to the unimportance of the country. Holland will and must also, notwithstanding the prosperity of her colonies, continue to decline, because the nation is too weak to support the enormous expense of a considerable military and naval power. Through her exertions to maintain her nationality Holland must become more and more deeply involved in debt. Notwithstanding her great colonial prosperity, she is and remains all the same a country dependent on England, and by her seeming independence she only strengthens the English supremacy. This is also the secret reason why England at the congress of Vienna took under her protection the restoration of the Dutch seeming independence. The case is exactly the same as with the Hanse Towns. On the side of England, Holland is a satellite for the English fleet — unite it with Germany, she is the leader of the German naval power. In her present position Holland cannot nearly so well derive profit from her colonial possessions as if they became a constituent part of the German Union, especially because she is too weak in the elements which are necessary for colonisation — in population and in mental powers. Further than this, the profitable development of her colonies, so far as that has hitherto been effected, depends for the most part on German good nature, or rather on the nonacquaintance of the Germans with their own national commercial interests; for while all other nations reserve their market for colonial produce for their own colonies and for the countries subject to them, the German market is the only one which remains open to the Dutch for the disposal of their surplus colonial produce. As soon as the Germans clearly comprehend that those from whom they purchase colonial produce must be made to understand that they on their part must purchase manufactured goods from Germany under differentially favourable treatment, then the Germans will also clearly see that they have it in their power to compel Holland to join the Zollverein. That union would be of the greatest advantage to both countries. Germany would give Holland the means not only of deriving profit from her colonies far better than at present, but also to found and to acquire new colonies. Germany would grant special perferential privileges to the Dutch and Hanseatic shipping, and grant special preferential privileges to Dutch colonial produce in the German markets. Holland and the Hanse Towns, in return, would preferentially export German manufactures, and preferentially employ their surplus capital in the manufactories and the agriculture of the interior of Germany.

Holland , as she has sunk from her eminence as a commercial power because she, the mere fraction of a nation, wanted to make herself pass as an entire nation; because she sought her advantage in the oppression and the weakening of the productive powers of Germany , instead of basing her greatness on the prosperity of the countries which lie behind her, with which every maritime state must stand or fall; because she sought to become great by her separation from the German nation instead of by her union with it; Holland can only again attain to her ancient state of prosperity by means of the German Union and in the closest connection with it. Only by this union is it possible to constitute an agricultural manufacturing commercial nationality of the first magnitude.

Dr Bowring groups in his tables the imports and exports of the German Customs Union with the Hanse Towns and Holland and Belgium all together, and from this grouping it clearly appears how greatly all these countries are dependent on the English manufacturing industry, and how immeasurably they might gain in their entire productive power by union. He estimates the imports of these countries from England at 19,842,121 l. sterling of official value, or 8,550,347 l. of declared value, but the exports of those countries to England (on the other hand) at only 4,804,491 l. sterling; in which, by the way, are included the great quantities of Java coffee, cheese, butter, &c. which England imports from Holland. These totals speak volumes. We thank the Doctor for his statistical grouping together — would that it might betoken a speedy political grouping.

NOTES:

1. Report on the German Zollverein to Lord Viscount Palmerston, by John Bowring, 1840.

2. See statement of R. B. Porter, note to p. 299.

Chapter 35

Continental Politics

The highest ultimate aim of rational politics is (as we have shown in our Second Book) the uniting of all nations under a common law of right, an object which is only to be attained through the greatest possible equalisation of the most important nations of the earth in civilisation, prosperity, industry, and power, by the conversion of the antipathies and conflicts which now exist between them into sympathy and harmony. But the solution of this problem is a work of immensely long duration. At the present time the nations are divided and repelled from one another by manifold causes; chief among these are conflicts about territory. As yet, the apportionment of territory to the European nations does not correspond to the nature of things. Indeed, even in theory, people are not yet agreed upon the fundamental conditions of a just and natural apportionment of territory. Some desire that their national territory should be determined according to the requirements of their metropolis without regard to language, commerce, race, and so forth, in such a way that the metropolis should be situated in the centre and be protected as much as possible against foreign attacks. They desire to have great rivers for their frontiers. Others maintain, and apparently with greater reason, that sea-coasts, mountains, language, and race, constitute better frontiers than great rivers. There still are nations who are not in possession of those mouths of rivers and sea-coasts which are indispensable to them for the development of their commerce with the world and for their naval power.

If every nation was already in possession of the territory which is necessary for its internal development, and for the maintenance of its political, industrial, and commercial independence, then every conquest of territory would be contrary to sound policy, because by the unnatural increase of territory the jealousy of the nation which is thus encroached upon would be excited and kept alive, and consequently the sacrifices which the conquering nation would have to make for retaining such provinces would be immeasurably greater than the advantages accruing from their possession. A just and wise apportionment of territory is, however, at this day not to be thought of, because this question is complicated by manifold interests of another nature. At the same time it must not be ignored that rectification of territory must be reckoned among the most important requirements of the nations, that striving to attain it is legitimate, that indeed in many cases it is a justifiable reason for war.

Further causes of antipathy between the nations are, at the present time, the diversity of their interests in respect to manufactures, commerce, navigation, naval power, and colonial possessions, also the difference in their degrees of civilisation, of religion, and of political condition. All these interests are complicated in manifold ways through the interests of dynasties and powers.

The causes of antipathy are, on the other hand, causes of sympathy. The less powerful nations sympathise against the most powerful, those whose independence is endangered sympathise against the aggressors, territorial powers against naval supremacy, those whose industry and commerce are defective sympathise against those who are striving for an industrial and commercial monopoly, the half-civilised against the civilised, those who are subjects of a monarchy against those whose government is entirely or partially democratic.

Nations at this time pursue their own interests and sympathies by means of alliances of those who are like-minded and have like interests against the interests and tendencies which conflict with theirs. As, however, these interests and tendencies conflict with one another in various ways, these alliances are liable to change. Those nations who are friends to-day may be enemies to-morrow, and vice versâ, as soon as ever some one of the great interests or principles is at stake by which they feel themselves repelled from or drawn towards one another.

Politicians have long felt that the equalisation of the nations must be their ultimate aim. That which people call the maintenance of the European balance of power has always been nothing else than the endeavours of the less powerful to impose a check on the encroachments of the more powerful. Yet politics have not seldom confounded their proximate object with their ultimate one, and vice versâ.

The proximate task of politics always consists in clearly perceiving in what respect the alliance and equalisation of the different interests is at the moment most pressing, and to strive that until this equalisation is attained all other questions may be suspended and kept in the background.

When the dynastic, monarchic, and aristocratic interests of Europe allied themselves against the revolutionary tendencies of 1789, disregarding all considerations regarding power and commerce, their policy was a correct one.

It was just as correct when the French Empire introduced the tendency of conquest in place of that of revolution.

Napoleon sought by his Continental system to establish a Continental coalition against the predominant naval and commercial power of England; but in order to succeed, it was necessary for him, first of all, to take away from the Continental nations the apprehension of being conquered by France. He failed, because on their part the fear of his supremacy on land greatly outweighed the disadvantages which they suffered from the naval supremacy.

With the fall of the French Empire, the object of the great alliance ceased. From that time forth, the Continental powers were menaced neither by the revolutionary tendencies nor by the lust of conquest of France. England's predominance in manufactures, navigation, commerce, colonial possessions, and naval power, had, on the other hand, enormously increased during the conflicts against the Revolution and against the French conquest. From that time forth, it became the interest of the Continental powers to ally themselves with France against the commercial and naval predominance. Solely from fear of the skin of the dead lion, the Continental powers did not heed sufficiently the living leopard who had hitherto fought in their ranks. The Holy Alliance was a political error.

This error also brought about its own punishment through the revolution of Italy. The Holy Alliance had unnecessarily called into life a counter force which no longer existed, or which at least would not for a long time have revived again. Fortunately for the Continental powers, the dynasty of July contrived to appease the revolutionary tendency in France. France concluded the alliance with England in the interests of the dynasty of July and of strengthening the constitutional monarchy. England concluded it in the interest of the maintenance of her commercial supremacy.

The Franco-English alliance ceased as soon as ever the dynasty of July and the constitutional monarchy in France felt themselves to be sufficiently firmly established; but, on the other hand, the interests of France in respect of naval power, navigation, commerce, industry, and foreign possessions came again more to the front. It is clear that France has again an equal interest with the other Continental powers in these questions, and the establishing of a Continental alliance against the naval predominance of England appears to be becoming a question of the day, provided the dynasty of July can succeed in creating perfect unity of will between the different organs of State administration, also to thrust into the background those territorial questions which are excited by the revolutionary tendencies, and entirely to appease in the minds of the monarchical Continental powers the fear of the tendencies of France towards revolution and aggression.

Nothing, however, at this time so greatly impedes a closer union of the continent of Europe as the fact that the centre of it still never takes the position for which it is naturally fitted. Instead of being a mediator between the east and the west of that continent, on all questions of arrangement of territory, of the principle of their constitutions, of national independence and power, for which it is qualified by its geographical position, by its federal constitution which excludes all apprehension of aggression in the minds of neighbouring nations, by its religious toleration, and its cosmopolitical tendencies, and finally by its civilisation and the elements of power which it possesses, this central part of Europe constitutes at present the apple of discord for which the east and the west contend, while each party hopes to draw to its own side this middle power, which is weakened by want of national unity, and is always uncertainly wavering hither and thither.

If, on the other hand, Germany could constitute itself with the   maritime territories which appertain to it, with Holland, Belgium, and Switzerland, as a powerful commercial and political whole — if this mighty national body could fuse representative institutions with the existing monarchical, dynastic, and aristocratic interests, so far as these are compatible with one another — then Germany could secure peace to the continent of Europe for a long time, and at the same time constitute herself the central point of a durable Continental alliance.

That the naval power of England greatly exceeds that of all other nations, if not on the number of ships, yet certainly in fighting power — that hence the nations which are less powerful at sea can only match England at sea by uniting their own naval power, is clear. From hence it follows, that every nation which is less powerful at sea has an interest in the maintenance and prosperity of the naval power of all other nations who are similarly weak at sea; and further, that fractions of other nations which, hitherto divided, have possessed either no naval power whatever or only an unimportant one, should constitute themselves into one united naval power. In regard to England, France and North America sustain loss if the naval power of Russia declines, and vice versâ. They all gain, if Germany, Holland, and Belgium constitute together a common naval power; for while separated these last are mere satellites to the supremacy of England, but if united they strengthen the opposition to that supremacy of all nations at sea.

None of these less powerful nations possesses a mercantile marine which exceeds the requirements of its own international trade — none of these nations possesses a manufacturing power which would maintain important preponderance over that of the others. None of them, therefore, has any ground to fear the competition of the others. On the other hand, all have a common interest in protecting themselves against the destructive competition of England. Hence it must be to the interests of all that the predominating manufacturing power of England should lose those means of access (Holland, Belgium, and the

Hanse Towns) by means of which England has hitherto dominated the markets of the Continent.

Inasmuch as the products of tropical climates are chiefly paid for by the manufactured products of temperate climates, and hence the consumption of the former depends on the sale of the latter, therefore every manufacturing nation should endeavour to establish direct intercourse with tropical countries. And thus, if all manufacturing nations of the second rank understand their own interests and act accordingly, no nation will be permitted to maintain a predominant amount of colonial possessions in tropical countries. If, for instance, England could succeed in the object for which she is at present striving, viz. to produce in India the colonial produce which she requires — in that case England could only carry on trade with the West Indies to the extent to which she was able to sell to other countries the colonial produce which she now obtains from the West Indies in exchange for her manufactured goods. If, however, she could not dispose of these to other countries, then her West Indian possessions would become useless to her. She would then have no other option than either to let them go free, or to surrender the trade with them to other manufacturing countries. Hence it follows that all manufacturing nations less powerful at sea have a common interest in following this policy and in reciprocally supporting one another in it, and it follows further that no one of these nations would lose by the accession of Holland to the German Commercial Union, and through the closer connection of Germany with the Dutch colonies.

Since the emancipation of the Spanish and Portuguese colonies in South America and the West Indies, it is no longer indispensably necessary that a manufacturing nation should possess colonies of its own in tropical climates in order to put itself in a position to carry on directly the exchange of manufactured goods against colonial produce. As the markets of these emancipated tropical countries are free, every manufacturing nation which is able to compete in these free markets can carry on direct trade with them. But these free tropical countries can only produce great quantities of colonial products, and only consume great quantities of manufactured goods, if prosperity and morality, peace and repose, lawful order and religious tolerance, prevail within them. All nations not powerful at sea, especially those who possess no colonies, or only unimportant ones, have hence a common interest in bringing about such a state of things by their united power. To England, with her commercial supremacy, the circumstances of these countries cannot matter so much because she is sufficiently supplied, or at least hopes to become sufficiently supplied, with colonial produce from her own exclusive and subject markets in the East and West Indies. From this point of view also we must partly judge respecting the extremely important question of slavery. We are very far from ignoring that much philanthropy and good motive lies at the root of the zeal with which the object of the emancipation of the negroes is pursued by England, and that this zeal does great honour to the character of the English nation. But at the same time, if we consider the immediate effects of the measures adopted by England in reference to this matter, we cannot get rid of the idea that also much political motive and commercial interest are mingled with it. These effects are: (1) That by the sudden emancipation of the blacks, through their rapid transition from a condition of disorder and carelessness little removed from that of wild animals to a high degree of individual independence, the yield of tropical produce of South America and the West Indies will be extremely diminished and ultimately reduced to nothing, as the example of St. Domingo incontestably shows, inasmuch as there since the expulsion of the French and Spaniards the production has greatly decreased from year to year, and continues to do so. (2) That the free negroes continually seek to obtain an increase in their wages, whilst they limit their labour to the supply of their most indispensable wants; that hence their freedom merely leads to idleness. (3) That, on the other hand, England possesses in the East Indies ample means for supplying the whole world with colonial products. It is well known that the Hindoos, owing to great industry and great moderation in their food and other wants, especially in consequence of the precepts of their religion, which forbid the use of animal food, are excessively frugal. To these must be added the want of capital among the natives, the great fruitfulness of the soil in vegetable products, and the restriction of caste and the great competition of those in want of work.

The result of all this is, that wages in India are incomparably lower than in the West Indies and South America, whether the plantations there are cultivated by free blacks or by slaves; that consequently the production of India, after trade has been set free in that country, and wiser principles of administration have prevailed, must increase at an enormous rate, and the time is no longer distant when England will not only be able to supply all her own requirements of colonial produce from India, but also export great quantities to other countries. Hence it follows that England cannot lose through the diminution of production in the West Indies and South America, to which countries other nations also export manufactured goods, but she will gain if the colonial production in India becomes preponderant, which market England exclusively supplies with manufactured goods. (4) Finally, it may be asserted, that by the emancipation of the slaves England desires to hang a sword over the head of the North American slave states, which is so much the more menacing to the Union the more this emancipation extends and the wish is excited among the negroes of North America to partake of similar liberty. The question if rightly viewed must appear a philanthropical experiment of doubtful benefit towards those on whose behalf it was undertaken from motives of general philanthropy, but must in any case appear to those nations who rely on the trade with South America and the West Indies as not advantageous to them; and they may not unreasonably inquire: Whether a sudden transition from slavery to freedom may not prove more injurious to the negroes themselves than the maintenance of the existing state of things? — whether it may not be the task of several generations to educate the negroes (who are accustomed to an almost animal state of subjection) to habits of voluntary labour and thrift? — whether it might not better attain the object if the transition from slavery to freedom was made by the introduction of a mild form of serfdom, whereby at first some interest might be secured to the serf in the land which he cultivates, and a fair share of the fruits of his labour, allowing sufficient rights to the landlord in order to bind the serf to habits of industry and order? — whether such a condition would not be more desirable than that of a miserable, drunken, lazy, vicious, mendicant horde called free negroes, in comparison with which Irish misery in its most degraded form may be deemed a state of prosperity and civilisation? If, however, we are required to believe that the zeal of the English to make everything which exists upon earth partakers of the same degree of freedom which they possess themselves, is so great and irrepressible that they must be excused if they have forgotten that nature makes no advances by leaps and bounds, then we must venture to put the questions: Whether the condition of the lowest caste of the Hindoos is not much more wretched and intolerable than that of the

American negroes? — and how it happens that the philanthropic spirit of England has never been excited on behalf of
these most miserable of mankind? — how it happens that
English legislation has never intervened for their benefit? —
how it happens that England has been active enough in deriving means for her own enrichment out of this miserable state of
things, without thinking of any direct means of ameliorating it?

The English-Indian policy leads us to the Eastern question. If
we can dismiss from the politics of the day all that which at this
moment has reference to territorial conflicts, to the dynastic,
monarchic, aristocratic, and religious interests, and to the
circumstances of the various powers, it cannot be ignored that
the Continental powers have a great national economic interest
in common in the Eastern question. However successful the
present endeavours of the powers may be to keep this question
in the background for a time, it will continually again come to
the front with renewed force. It is a conclusion long arrived at
by all thoughtful men, that a nation so thoroughly undermined
in her religious, moral, social, and political foundations as
Turkey is, is like a corpse, which may indeed be held up for a
time by the support of the living, but must none the less pass
into corruption. The case is quite the same with the Persians as
with the Turks, with the Chinese and Hindoos and all other
Asiatic people. Wherever the mouldering civilisation of Asia
comes into contact with the fresh atmosphere of Europe, it falls
to atoms; and Europe will sooner or later find herself under the
necessity of taking the whole of Asia under her care and tute-
lage, as already India has been so taken in charge by England.
In this utter chaos of countries and peoples there exists no
single nationality which is either worthy or capable of maintenance and regeneration. Hence the entire dissolution of the
Asiatic nationalities appears to be inevitable, and a regenera-

tion of Asia only possible by means of an infusion of European vital power, by the general introduction of the Christian religion and of European moral laws and order, by European immigration, and the introduction of European systems of government.

If we reflect on the course which such a regeneration might possibly pursue, the first consideration that strikes one is that the greater part of the East is richly provided by nature with resources for supplying the manufacturing nations of Europe with great quantities of raw materials and necessary articles of every kind, but especially for producing tropical products, and in exchange for these for opening unlimited markets to European manufacturers. From this circumstance, nature appears to have given an indication that this regeneration, as generally is the case with the civilisation of barbarous peoples, must proceed by the path of free exchange of agricultural produce against manufactured goods. For that reason the principle must be firmly maintained above all by the European nations, that no exclusive commercial privileges must be reserved to any European nation in any part of Asia whatever, and that no nation must be favoured above others there in any degree. It would be especially advantageous to the extension of this trade, if the chief commercial emporiums of the East were constituted free cities, the European population of which should have the right of self-government in consideration of an annual payment of tax to the native rulers. But European agents should be appointed to reside with these rulers, after the example of English policy in India, whose advice the native rulers should be bound to follow in respect of the promotion of public security order, and civilisation.

All the Continental powers have especially a common interest that neither of the two routes from the Mediterranean to the Red Sea and to the Persian Gulf should fall into the exclusive possession of England, nor remain impassable owing to Asiatic barbarism. To commit the duty of protecting these important points to Austria, would insure the best guarantees to all European nations.

Further, the Continental powers in general have a common interest with the United States in maintaining the principle that 'free ships cover free goods,' and that only an effectual blockade of individual ports, but not a mere proclamation of the blockade of entire coasts, ought to be respected by neutrals. Finally, the principle of the annexation of wild and uninhabited territories appears to require revision in the common interest of the Continental powers. People ridicule in our days the fact that the Holy Father formerly undertook to make presents of islands and parts of the globe, nay even to divide the world into two parts with a stroke of the pen, and to apportion this part to one man and that to another. Can it, however, be deemed much more sensible to acknowledge the title to an entire quarter of the globe to vest in the man who first erected somewhere on the earth a pole adorned with a piece of silk? That in the case of islands of moderate size the right of the discoverer should be respected, may be admitted consistently with common sense; but when the question arises as to islands which are as large as a great European kingdom (like New Zealand) or respecting a continent which is larger than the whole of Europe (like Australia), in such a case by nothing less than an actual occupation by colonisation, and then only for the actually colonised territory, can a claim to exclusive possession be admitted consistently with common sense. And it is not clear why the Germans and the French should not have the right to found colonies in those parts of the world at points which are distant from the English stations.

If we only consider the enormous interests which the nations of the Continent have in common, as opposed to the English maritime supremacy, we shall be led to the conviction that nothing is so necessary to these nations as union, and nothing is so ruinous to them as Continental wars. The history of the last century also teaches us that every war which the powers of the Continent have waged against one another has had for its invariable result to increase the industry, the wealth, the navigation, the colonial possessions, and the power of the insular supremacy.

Hence, it cannot be denied that a correct view of the wants and interests of the Continent underlaid the Continental system of Napoleon, although it must not be ignored that Napoleon desired to give effect to this idea (right in itself) in a manner which was contrary to the independence and to the interests of the other Continental powers. The Continental system of Napoleon suffered from three capital defects. In the first place, it sought to establish, in the place of the English maritime supremacy, a French Continental supremacy; it sought the humiliation, or destruction and dissolution, of other nationalities on the Continent for the benefit of France, instead of basing itself on the elevation and equalisation of the other Continental nations. Furthermore, France followed herself an exclusive commercial policy against the other countries of the Continent, while she claimed for herself free competition in those countries. Finally, the system almost entirely destroyed the trade between the manufacturing countries of the Continent and tropical countries, and found itself compelled to find a remedy for the destruction of this international trade by the use of substituted articles.(1*)

That the idea of this Continental system will ever recur, that the necessity of realising it will the more forcibly impress itself on the Continental nations in proportion as the preponderance of England in industry, wealth, and power further increases, is already very clear, and will continually become more evident. But it is not less certain that an alliance of the Continental nations can only have a good result if France is wise enough to avoid the errors of Napoleon. Hence, it is foolish of France if she raises (contrary to all justice, and to the actual nature of circumstances) claims for extension of frontiers at the expense of Germany, and thereby compels other nations of the Continent to ally themselves with England.

It is foolish of France if she speaks of the Mediterranean Sea as of a French lake, and seeks to acquire exclusive influence in the Levant and in South America.

An effective Continental system can only originate from the free union of the Continental powers, and can succeed only in case it has for its object (and also effects) an equal participation in the advantages which result from it, for in that way only, and in no other, can the maritime powers of second rank command respect from the predominant power of England in such a way that the latter without any recourse to the force of arms will concede all the just requirements of the less powerful states. Only by such an alliance as that will the Continental manufacturing powers be able to maintain their relations with tropical countries, and assert and secure their interests in the East and the West.

In any case the British, who are ever too anxious for supremacy, must feel it hard when they perceive in this manner how the Continental nations will reciprocally raise their manufacturing power by mutual commercial concessions and by treaties; how they will reciprocally strengthen their navigation and their naval power; how they will assert their claim to that share for which they are fitted by nature in civilising and colonising barbarous and uncultivated countries, and in trade with tropical regions. Nevertheless, a glance into the future ought sufficiently to console the britons for these anticipated disadvantages.

For the same causes which have raised Great Britain to her present exalted position, will (probably in the course of the next century) raise the United States of America to a degree of industry, wealth, and power, which will surpass the position in which England stands, as far as at present England excels little Holland. In the natural course of things the United States will increase their population within that period to hundreds of millions of souls; they will diffuse their population, their institutions, their civilisation, and their spirit over the whole of Central and South America, just as they have recently diffused them over the neighbouring Mexican province. The Federal Union will comprise all these immense territories, a population of several hundred millions of people will develop the resources of a continent which infinitely exceeds the continent of Europe in extent and in natural wealth. The naval power of the western world will surpass that of Great Britain, as greatly as its coasts and rivers exceed those of Britain in extent and magnitude.

Thus in a not very distant future the natural necessity which now imposes on the French and Germans the necessity of establishing a Continental alliance against the British supremacy, will impose on the British the necessity of establishing a European coalition against the supremacy of America. Then will Great Britain be compelled to seek and to find in the leadership of the united powers of Europe protection, security, and compensation against the predominance of America, and an equivalent for her lost supremacy.

It is therefore good for England that she should practise

resignation betimes, that she should by timely renunciations gain the friendship of European Continental powers, that she should accustom herself betimes to the idea of being only the first among equals.

NOTES:

1. This fact is confirmed by Mad. Junot, in Mémoires de la Duchess d'Abrantès. — [TRANSLATOR.]

Chapter 36

The Commercial Policy of the German Zollverein

If any nation whatever is qualified for the establishment of a national manufacturing power, it is Germany; by the high rank which she maintains in science and art, in literature and education, in public administration and in institutions of public utility; by her morality and religious character, her industry and domestic economy; by her perseverance and steadfastness in business occupations; as also by her spirit of invention, by the number and vigour of her population; by the extent and nature of her territory, and especially by her highly advanced agriculture, and her physical, social, and mental resources.

If any nation whatever has a right to anticipate rich results from a protective system adapted to her circumstances, for the progress of her home manufactures, for the increase of her foreign trade and her navigation, for the perfecting of her internal means of transport, for the prosperity of her agriculture, as also for the maintenance of her independence and the increase of her power abroad, it is Germany.

Yes, we venture to assert, that on the development of the German protective system depend the existence, the independence and the future of the German nationality. Only in the soil of general prosperity does the national spirit strike its roots, produce fine blossoms and rich fruits; only from the unity of material interests does mental power arise, and only from both of these national power. But of what value are all our endeavours, whether we are rulers or subjects, nobles or simple citizens, learned men, soldiers, or civilians, manufacturers, agriculturists, or merchants, without nationality and without guarantees for the continuance of our nationality?

Meanwhile, however, the German protective system only accomplishes its object in a very imperfect manner, so long as Germany does not spin for herself the cotton and linen yarn which she requires; so long as she does not directly import from tropical countries the colonial produce which she requires, and pay for it with goods of her own manufacture; so long as she does not carry on this trade with her own ships; so long as she has no means of protecting her own flag; so long as she possesses no perfect system of transport by river, canal, or railway; so long as the German Zollverein does not include all German maritime territories and also Holland and belgium. We have treated these subjects circumstantially in various places in this book, and it is only necessary for us here to recapitulate what we have already thus treated.

If we import raw cotton from Egypt, Brazil, and North America, we in that case pay for it in our own manufactured goods; if, on the other hand, we import cotton yarn from England, we have to pay the value of it in raw materials and articles of food which we could more advantageously work up or consume ourselves, or else we must pay for it in specie which we have acquired elsewhere, and with which we could more advantageously purchase foreign raw materials to work up for ourselves, or colonial produce for our own consumption.

In the same way the introduction of spinning linen yarn by machinery offers us the means not only of increasing our home consumption of linen, and of perfecting our agriculture, but also of enormously increasing our trade with tropical countries.

For the two above-named branches of industry, as well as for the manufacture of woollens, we are as favourably circumstanced as any other nation, by an amount of water power hitherto not utilised, by cheap necessaries of life, and by low wages. What we lack is simply and solely a guarantee for our capitalists and artisans by which they may be protected against loss of capital and want of work. A moderate protective duty of about twenty-five per cent during the next five years, which could be maintained for a few years at that rate and then be lowered to fifteen to twenty per cent, ought completely to accomplish this object. Every argument which is adduced by the supporters of the theory of values against such a measure, has been refuted by us. On the other hand, we may add a further argument in favour of that measure, that these great branches of industry especially offer us the means for establishing extensive machine manufactories and for the development of a race of competent technical instructors and practical foremen.

In the trade in colonial produce Germany, as France and England have done, has to follow the principle — that in respect to the purchase of the colonial produce which we require, we should give a preference to those tropical countries which purchase manufactured goods from us; or, in short, that we should buy from those who buy from us. That is the case in reference to our trade with the West Indies and to North and South America.

But it is not yet the case in reference to our trade with Holland, which country supplies us with enormous quantities of her colonial produce, but only takes in return disproportionately small quantities of our manufactured goods.

At the same time Holland is naturally directed to the market of Germany for the disposal of the greater part of her colonial produce, inasmuch as England and France derive their supplies of such produce for the most part from their own colonies and from subject countries (where they exclusively possess the market for manufactured goods), and hence they only import small quantities of Dutch colonial produce.

Holland has no important manufacturing industry of her own, but, on the other hand, has a great productive industry in her colonies, which has recently greatly increased and may yet be immeasurably further increased. But Holland desires of Germany that which is unfair, and acts contrary to her own interests if rightly understood, inasmuch as she desires to dispose of the greater part of her colonial produce to Germany, while she desires to supply her requirements of manufactured goods from any quarter she likes best. This is, for Holland, an only apparently beneficial and a short-sighted policy; for if Holland would give preferential advantages to German manufactured goods both in the mother country and in her colonies, the demand in Germany for Dutch colonial produce would increase in the same proportion in which the sale of German manufactured goods to Holland and her colonies increased, or, in other words, Germany would be able to purchase so much the more colonial produce in proportion as she sold more manufactured goods to Holland; Holland would be able to dispose of so much more colonial produce to Germany as she purchased from Germany manufactured goods. This reciprocal exchange operation is, at present, rendered impracticable by Holland if she sells her colonial produce to Germany while she purchases her requirements in manufactured goods from England, because England (no matter how much of manufactured goods she sells to Holland) will always supply the greater part of her own requirements of colonial produce from her own colonies, or from the countries which are subject to her.

Hence the interests of Germany require that she should either demand from Holland a differential duty in favour of

Germany's manufacturing production, by which the latter can secure to herself the exclusive market for manufactured goods in Holland and her colonies, or, in case of refusal, that Germany should impose a differential duty on the import of colonial produce in favour of the produce of Central and South America and of the free markets of the West Indies.

The above-named policy would constitute the most effective means of inducing Holland to join the German Zollverein.

As matters now stand, Germany has no reason for sacrificing her own manufactories of beetroot sugar to the trade with Holland; for only in case Germany can pay for her requirements of this article by means of her own manufactured goods, is it more to her advantage to supply that requirement by an exchange trade with tropical countries, than by producing it herself at home.

Hence the attention of Germany should be at once chiefly directed to the extension of her trade with Northern, Central, and South America, and with the free markets of the West Indies. In connection with that, the following measures, in addition to that above adverted to, appear desirable: the establishment of a regular service of steamships between the German seaports and the principal ports of those countries, the promotion of emigration thither, the confirmation and extension of friendly relations between them and the Zollverein, and especially the promotion of the civilisation of those countries.

Recent experience has abundantly taught us how enormously commerce on a large scale is promoted by a regular service of steamships. France and belgium are already treading in the footsteps of England in this respect, as they well perceive that every nation which is behindhand in this more perfect means of transport must retrograde in her foreign trade. The German seaports also have already recognised this; already one public company has been completely formed in Bremen for building two or three steam vessels for the trade with the United States. This, however, is clearly an insufficient provision. The commercial interests of Germany require not only a regular service of steam vessels with North America, especially with New York, Boston, Charleston, and New Orleans, but also with Cuba, San Domingo, and Central and South America. Germany ought to be behind no other nation in respect to these latter lines of steam navigation. It must certainly not be ignored that the means which are required for these objects will be too great for the spirit of enterprise, and perhaps also for the power of the German seaports, and it seems to us they can only be carried into effect by means of liberal subsidies on the part of the states of the Zollverein. The prospect of such subsidies as well as of differential duties in favour of German shipping, ought at once to constitute a strong motive for these seaports to become included in the Commercial Union. When one considers how greatly the exports of manufactured goods and the imports of colonial produce, and consequently also the customs revenue, of the states of the Zollverein would be increased by such a measure, one cannot doubt that even a considerable expenditure for this object must appear as only a reproductive investment of capital from which rich returns are to be expected.

Through the increase of the means of intercourse of Germany with the above-named countries, the emigration of Germans to those countries and their settlement there as citizens would be no less promoted; and by that means the foundation would be laid for future increase of commerce with them. For this object the states of the Zollverein ought to establish everywhere consulates and diplomatic agencies, by means of which the settlement and undertakings of German citizens could be promoted, and especially to assist those states in every practicable way in giving stability to their governments and improving their degree of civilisation.

We do not share in the least the opinion of those who think that the tropical countries of America offer less advantages to German colonisation than those of temperate climate in North America. However great, as we have openly confessed, is our attachment for the last-named country, and however little we are able or desire to deny that an individual German emigrant who possesses a little capital has greater hope of permanently making his fortune in Western North America, we must nevertheless here express our opinion that emigration to Central and South America, if it were well led and undertaken on a large scale, offers in a national point of view much greater advantages for Germany than emigration to North America. What good is it if the emigrants to North America become ever so prosperous? In their personal relation they are lost for ever to the German nationality, and also from their material production Germany can expect only unimportant fruits. It is a pure delusion if people think that the German language can be maintained by the Germans who live in the interior of the United States, or that after a time it may be possible to establish entire German states there. We once ourselves entertained this illusion, but after ten years' observation in the country itself, on the spot, we have entirely given it up. It lies in the very spirit of every nationality, and above all in that of the United States, to assimilate itself in language, literature, administration, and legislation; and it is good that that is so. However many Germans may now be living in North America, yet certainly not one of them is living there whose great-grandchildren will not greatly prefer the English language to the German, and that for the very natural reason that the former is the language of the

119

educated people, of the literature, the legislation, the administration, the courts of justice, and the trade and commerce of the country. The same thing can and will happen to the Germans in North America as happened to the Huguenots in Germany and the French in Louisiana. They naturally must and will be amalgamated with the predominant population: some a little sooner, others a little later, according as they dwell more or less together with fellow-countrymen.

Still less dependence can be placed on an active intercourse between Germany and the German emigrants to the west of North America. The first settler is always compelled by necessity to make for himself the greater part of his articles of clothing and utensils; and these customs, which originated from mere necessity, continue for the most part to the second and third generation. Hence it is that North America itself is a country which makes powerful efforts in manufacturing industry, and will continually strive more and more to gain possession of her home market for manufactured goods, for her own industry.

On the other hand, we would on that account by no means maintain that the American market for manufactured goods is not a very important one, and well worthy of regard, especially for Germany On the contrary, we are of opinion that for many articles of luxury and for manufactured articles which are easy of transport, and in which the wages of labour constitute a chief element of the price, that market is one of the most important, and must from year to year, as respects the articles above named, become more important for Germany. What we contend is only this, that those Germans who emigrate to the west of North America give no important assistance in increasing the demand for German manufactured goods, and that in reference to that object emigration to Central and South America requires and deserves very much more direct encouragement.

The above-mentioned countries, including Texas, are for the most part adapted for raising colonial produce. They can and will never make great progress in manufacturing industry. Here there is an entirely new and rich market for manufactured goods to acquire; whoever has here established firm commercial relations, may remain in possession of them for all future time. These countries, without sufficient moral power of their own to raise themselves to a higher grade of civilisation, to introduce well-ordered systems of government, and to endue them with stability, will more and more come to the conviction that they must be aided from outside, namely, by immigration. In these quarters the English and French are hated on account of their arrogance, and owing to jealousy for national independence — the Germans for the opposite reasons are liked. Hence the states of the Zollverein ought to devote the closest attention to these countries.

A vigorous German consular and diplomatic system ought to be established in these quarters, the branches of which should enter into correspondence with one another. Young explorers should be encouraged to travel through these countries and make impartial reports upon them. Young merchants should be encouraged to inspect them — young medical men to go and practise there. Companies should be founded and supported by actual share subscription, and taken under special protection, which companies should be formed in the German seaports in order to buy large tracts of land in those countries and to settle them with German colonists — companies for commerce and navigation, whose object should be to open new markets in those countries for German manufactures and to establish lines of steamships — mining companies, whose object should be to devote German knowledge and industry to winning the great mineral wealth of those countries. In every possible way the Zollverein ought to endeavour to gain the good-will of the population and also of the governments of those countries, and especially to promote by that means public security means of communication, and public order; indeed, one ought not to hesitate, in case one could by that means put the governments of those countries under obligation to us, also to assist them by sending an important auxiliary corps.

A similar policy ought to be followed in reference to the East — to European Turkey and the Lower Danubian territories. Germany has an immeasurable interest that security and order should be firmly established in those countries, and in no direction so much as in this is the emigration of Germans so easy for individuals to accomplish, or so advantageous for the nation. A man dwelling by the Upper Danube could transport himself to Moldavia and Wallachia, to Servia, or also to the south-western shores of the Black Sea, for one-fifth part of the expenditure of money and time which are requisite for his emigration to the shores of Lake Erie. What attracts him to the latter more than to the former is, the greater degree of liberty, security, and order which prevails in the latter. But under the existing circumstances of Turkey it ought not to be impossible to the German states, in alliance with Austria, to exercise such an influence on the improvement of the public condition of those countries, that the German colonist should no longer feel himself repelled from them, especially if the governments themselves would found companies for colonisation, take part in them themselves, and grant them continually their special protection.

In the meantime it is clear that settlements of this kind could only have a specially beneficial effect on the industry of the states of the Zollverein, if no obstacles were placed in the way of the exchange of German manufactured goods for the agricultural produce of the colonists, and if that exchange was promoted by cheap and rapid means of communication. Hence it is to the interest of the states of the Zollverein, that Austria should facilitate as much as possible the through traffic on the Danube, and that steam navigation on the Danube should be roused to vigorous activity —consequently that it should at the outset be actually subsidised by the Governments.

Especially, nothing is so desirable as that the Zollverein and Austria at a later period, after the industry of the Zollverein states has been better developed and has been placed in a position of greater equality to that of Austria, should make, by means of a treaty, reciprocal concessions in respect to their manufactured products.

After the conclusion of such a treaty, Austria would have an equal interest with the states of the Zollverein in making the Turkish provinces available for the benefit of their manufacturing industry and of their foreign commerce.

In anticipation of the inclusion in the Zollverein of the German seaports and Holland, it would be desirable that Prussia should now make a commencement by the adoption of a German commercial flag, and by laying the foundation for a future German fleet, and that she should try whether and how German colonies can be founded in Australia, New Zealand, or in or on other islands of Australasia.

The means for such attempts and commencements, and for the undertakings and subventions which we have previously recommended as desirable, must be acquired in the same way in which England and France have acquired the means of supporting their foreign commerce and their colonisation and of maintaining their powerful fleets, namely, by imposing duties on the imports of colonial produce. United action, order, and energy could be infused into these measures of the Zollverein, if the Zollverein states would assign the direction of them in respect to the North and transmarine affairs to Prussia, and in respect to the Danube and Oriental affairs to Bavaria. An addition of ten per cent to the present import duties on manufactures and colonial produce would at present place one million and a half per annum at the disposal of the Zollverein. And as it may be expected with certainty, as a result of the continual increase in the export of manufactured goods, that in the course of time consumption of colonial produce in the states of the Zollverein will increase to double and treble its present amount, and consequently their customs revenue will increase in like proportion, sufficient provision will be made for satisfying the requirements above mentioned, if the states of the Zollverein establish the principle that over and above the addition of ten per cent a part also of all future increase in import duties should be placed at the disposal of the Prussian Government to be expended for these objects.

As regards the establishment of a German transport system, and especially of a German system of railways, we beg to refer to a work of our own which specially treats of that subject. This great enterprise will pay for itself, and all that is required of the Governments can be expressed in one word, and that is — ENERGY.

COSIMO CLASSICS

COSIMO is an innovative publisher of books and publications that inspire, inform and engage readers worldwide. Our titles are drawn from a range of subjects including health, business, philosophy, history, science and sacred texts. We specialize in using print-on-demand technology (POD), making it possible to publish books for both general and specialized audiences and to keep books in print indefinitely. With POD technology new titles can reach their audiences faster and more efficiently than with traditional publishing.

> ➢ **Permanent Availability:** Our books & publications never go out-of-print.

> ➢ **Global Availability:** Our books are always available online at popular retailers and can be ordered from your favorite local bookstore.

COSIMO CLASSICS brings to life unique, rare, out-of-print classics representing subjects as diverse as *Alternative Health, Business and Economics, Eastern Philosophy, Personal Growth, Mythology, Philosophy, Sacred Texts, Science, Spirituality* and much more!

COSIMO-on-DEMAND publishes your books, publications and reports. If you are an Author, part of an Organization, or a Benefactor with a publishing project and would like to bring books back into print, publish new books fast and effectively, would like your publications, books, training guides, and conference reports to be made available to your members and wider audiences around the world, we can assist you with your publishing needs.

Visit our website at www.cosimobooks.com to learn more about Cosimo, browse our catalog, take part in surveys or campaigns, and sign-up for our newsletter.

And if you wish please drop us a line at info@cosimobooks.com. We look forward to hearing from you.

Printed in the United Kingdom by
Lightning Source UK Ltd., Milton Keynes
139070UK00001B/38/A